PENGI

TRAC

Prosenjit Das Gupta was educated at St Xavier's Collegiate School and Presidency College in Calcutta. He has been in service in trade and industry since 1966. Das Gupta's articles on folk crafts and wildlife conservation have appeared in several leading newspapers and magazines. He has a keen interest in photography and travel, and is the author of *10 Walks in Calcutta* and *Walks in the Wild*.

Tracking Jim

A Hunt in Corbett Country

PROSENJIT DAS GUPTA

PENGUIN BOOKS

PENGUIN BOOKS
Published by the Penguin Group
Penguin Books India Pvt. Ltd, 11 Community Centre, Panchsheel Park,
New Delhi 110 017, India
Penguin Group (USA) Inc., 375 Hudson Street, New York, NY 10014, USA
Penguin Group (Canada), 10 Alcorn Avenue, Toronto, Ontario, Canada
M4V 3B2 (a division of Pearson Penguin Canada Inc.)
Penguin Books Ltd, 80 Strand, London WC2R 0RL, England
Penguin Ireland, 25 St Stephen's Green, Dublin 2, Ireland (a division of
Penguin Books Ltd)
Penguin Group (Australia), 250 Camberwell Road, Camberwell, Victoria
3124, Australia (a division of Pearson Australia Group Pty Ltd)
Penguin Group (NZ), cnr Airborne and Rosedale Roads, Albany, Auckland
1310, New Zealand (a division of Pearson New Zealand Ltd)
Penguin Group (South Africa) (Pty) Ltd, 24 Sturdee Avenue, Rosebank,
Johannesburg 2196, South Africa

Penguin Books Ltd, Registered Offices: 80 Strand, London WC2R 0RL,
England

First published by Penguin Books India 2005
Copyright © Prosenjit Das Gupta 2005

10 9 8 7 6 5 4 3 2 1

Typeset in Sabon by InoSoft Systems, Noida
Printed at Chaman Offset Printers, New Delhi

To Kumaon and the memory of Jim Corbett

Contents

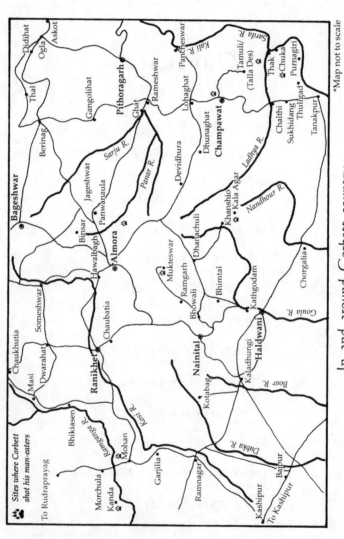

In and around Corbett country

*Map not to scale

Sites where Corbett
shot his man-eaters

Preface

What *is* so special about Jim Corbett that impels people to write about him or to try and obtain insights into the persona of this intensely private man?

The cursory facts of his life and career in India and Africa are there on record. Born in 1875, Corbett served in the railways, spent some years in East Africa, administered a small village in the foothills of Kumaon and was famous for hunting and killing man-eating tigers and leopards.

But the many reasons that have fed my fascination for him from the time I was a child lie elsewhere: firstly, in the raw courage that had spurred him on to stalk and kill eight man-eating tigers and two man-eating leopards whose depredations had wreaked havoc on rural life in parts of Kumaon during the first few decades of the twentieth century; secondly, in his ability to create vivid word-pictures of the region's hills and forests and to bring alive the tense moments he spent in pursuit of man-eaters during which his skills and limited knowledge of the forest were pitted against the knife-edged primal instincts of ferocious carnivores; and thirdly, in his command over the language of the Indian jungles, as evident in the calls of the wild animals that animate them as in the message of the tell-tale tracks left on dusty trails. It was only when I visited the Indian jungles once frequented by Corbett that his observations acquired immediacy and a new relevance. Another aspect of his personality that appealed to me immensely while reading his writings was his very humanity, apparent in his concerns, his pleasures and his vulnerabilities.

This book is intended, primarily, as an acknowledgement of my remembrance of and respect for Jim Corbett. It also chronicles, in a sense, my own journey into the life and personality of the man, based on clues picked up from his writings as well as from reminiscences of those who had met him in the 1940s. Equally, it is the story of actual journeys that I undertook into unknown areas far away from home, into experiences that would not only lead me into the heart of Corbett country but also establish, albeit vicariously, a kind of intimacy with the man who has left his indelible mark on it.

I have tried to share with the reader whatever I saw and sensed on the ground, besides the experiences culled from Corbett's own books and from other references. Hence the brief outlines I have given of Corbett's accounts of his pursuit of the man-eaters are complemented by descriptions of my own explorations, so many years later, in the hunter's wake. My aim is to place my narrative in perspective, lend it a sense of order and highlight certain features of the hunter's psyche. This is followed by short sketches intended to bring out those aspects of Corbett's personality and capabilities which made him what he was. The objective is to work towards a fuller portrait of the man, lending him greater depth and dimension, without destroying the enigma that is part of his legend.

I sincerely hope these notes will be of interest to those who have enjoyed Corbett's books and are keen to know more about the man who wrote them. If this book succeeds in encouraging more people to peruse the Book of Nature, of which Corbett himself was such an avid reader, it would be the best tribute to the man and his unforgettable myth.

Prosenjit Das Gupta

Acknowledgements

Writing about a person who lived about seventy or eighty years ago and who had left this country more than half a century earlier leaving behind little record of his life is no small task. Fortunately, there are people around in Nainital and elsewhere who still remember Jim Corbett from the 1940s. Their recollections and the detailed descriptions of the locations, as well as the hints and inferences gleaned from Corbett's own writings by the process of picking up tracks that he had turned into a fine art, have helped me a great deal.

The biographies of Corbett by D.C. Kala (*Jim Corbett of Kumaon*, 1979) and Martin Booth (*Carpet Sahib*, 1987) have been most useful in providing the basic facts about the hunter's life. They would serve, I am sure, as important references on Corbett for quite some time to come. At the same time, their writings inspired me to learn more about the man in my own fashion, especially with regard to certain aspects of his personality that had not been fully discussed, and also to give the reader a feel of the lay of the land should he take it into his head to 'discover' Corbett and Kumaon.

I am deeply grateful to Mr P.K. Verma for allowing me to visit Gurney House in Nainital and to permit the reproduction of a couple of the pictures here. I am also beholden to him and to Mrs Kiran Verma and Mrs Jyotsna Sinha for so readily giving their time to deal with my constant questioning. I sincerely acknowledge their contribution in making Corbett something more than just a name on the cover of a book. I am also obliged to the forest department staff for showing me around Kaladhungi and Corbett's house in the village. The lively discussions with Deb-ban Goswami, son of Bara Punvan (or Panwa, as he was affectionately called by Corbett), were useful in filling in the local colour.

I must place on record my deep gratitude to Dr Chris Mills of the Photo-Films Division at the library of the Natural History Museum in London for sparing his valuable time to locate and to show me the films taken by Corbett that are still stored there.

I would be failing in my duty if I did not thank Diya Kar Hazra of Penguin India for getting the book going and acknowledge the fine editorial contributions of Mita Ghose and Poulomi Chatterjee. I would also like to thank Pritam Chatterjee for his assistance with the map and photographs.

In a way, the biggest debt of gratitude I owe is to Kumaon for protecting in the folds of her hills the forests, rivers, streams, villages and the people among whom Jim Corbett lived and hunted. I was able to observe and experience some of the things that Corbett had himself seen and written of fifty years ago. I am sure that had he been able to bridge the past and the present Corbett would have liked to see the Ramganga, the Nandhour and the Sarda rivers in the 1990s much the way they used to be in the 1930s, clothed in deep forests and still running with mahseer, and to listen once again to the alarm call of the kakar and the chital on the banks of the Boar.

Beginnings

Illness is a bore for anyone at the best of times. So it doesn't require much imagination to understand how much worse it could be for a child forced to languish in bed with a thermometer thrust under his tongue at regular intervals, while important classes, the rough and tumble of the football field in the afternoons and savouries from the school tuck shop lie just beyond his reach.

During my own recurring bouts of illness throughout my childhood, my only real consolation lay in listening to the thrilling stories about my maternal grandfather and the years he spent in the forests of the North East, when he was posted in the area on official work. They were narrated to me umpteen times by my grandmother, a small, almost fragile woman, lit up from within, it seemed, by some inner flame that had borne her through more than forty arduous years of sharing life in the wild with her husband, even as she raised her family. Set in the areas around Dibrugarh in Upper Assam (including the fabled Subansiri gorge), near Kokrajhar, at Tura in the Garo Hills and in the Chakrata hills, those tales of hunting and fishing from the decade beginning in 1910 and spilling over into the 1920s retained nearly all their magic despite the countless retellings.

There were further, delightful diversions from the vicious cycle of thermometer, medicine and injection: the stories from Jim Corbett's *Man-Eaters of Kumaon*, read aloud to me by an aunt. She had spent a good part of her early life in or near jungles with my grandfather and had a way of imbuing with uncanny realism her descriptions of the pug marks of a tiger padding along a jungle path, the alarm call of the langur and the kakar or the scratching of jungle fowl in the undergrowth. The episode of the Chowgarh tigers, for instance, in which Corbett finally caught up with the man-eater—or was it the other way round?—will be etched in my subconscious forever.

The thrill inherent in this kind of 'participatory reading' was not mine alone; my cousins, familiar with the most intricate details of Corbett lore, shared it with me and we often engaged in feverish arguments on this or that detail about a particular Corbett story. Our interest in the ways of the jungle, especially in tales involving the hunting of man-eating tigers by Corbett, found expression in the games we enjoyed as children. Along with a handful of willing cousins, I would enter with enthusiasm into the game of shikar. In a particular variant of this game, one of us would be 'tagged' as the tiger. He had to track down the others, locating their whereabouts from the sound of knees knocking against the bedpost, the pitter-patter of bare feet on the tiled floor, the swish of curtains being pushed aside and the suppressed coughs and giggles. Then the 'tiger' would charge and cause a mad stampede around the bedstead or the drawing room settee. Besides the chance of some innocent rough-housing which it afforded us, the game helped attune our ears to the direction and distance of sounds. Another version of the game was more complex. It involved acting out a shikar and required elaborate arrangements to create the right atmosphere. One of my cousins would be chosen to play the tiger. He would pad up and down the 'game track' beside the bed, growling in undertones or snarling viciously as he stalked the 'tent'—a bedcover draped over an umbrella under which the 'shikaris' huddled together. Each growl and snarl would be greeted by shrieks of pleasurable fear from the 'shikaris' in the tent and there would be furious attempts to aim the 'rifle', usually a badminton racquet, at the 'tiger'. Tiring after a while of the 'missed' shots taken at random, the 'tiger' would attack the tent with loud snarls. The game would be over if the 'tiger' succeeded in making a sudden dash for one of the 'victims' and snatching away the 'rifle'. The session always ended with the 'tiger' and the 'shikaris' sitting amicably together and sharing the pastries and cookies they had cadged from their aunts as 'rations' while preparing for the 'hunt'!

As I look back on those games, I realize that while they were based on the mistaken assumption that tigers are inevitably bloodthirsty and lurk behind every other bush waiting to pounce on unsuspecting humans, they did have certain positive aspects. They taught us how to decipher shapes in the half-light and got us accustomed to putting a rifle to our shoulders in faithful imitation of our elders. They also marked the birth of a passion, though I didn't know it then.

Passing out of school, getting through college and chalking out a career ensured that for the next decade or so Corbett's exploits and our imitation of them were reduced to little more than a vague memory. The occasional winter bird-shoots during the 1950s and 1960s offered us fleeting opportunities to feel the early morning chill seep up through the soles of our shoes, as the outlines of trees and bushes in the half-darkness turned hazier in the gathering mist and the dew dripped without pause from overhanging trees, much as Corbett had observed during the shoots near Garuppu in the 1890s. However, those moments were too few and far between to intervene in the daily grind of professional work and family preoccupations. At the same time, in hindsight, they seemed to have insinuated themselves into our consciousness, much as the calls of peafowl and jungle fowl in the forests around Kaladhungi had left their mark on Corbett.

It is true that while I had been caught up with life the embers of my unspoken admiration for the slayer of the man-eaters of Kumaon had burned low, but burn they did. It took just one visit to the Hazaribagh National Park in 1969 and a walk down the sal-shaded forest trails, looking out in the growing dusk for sambar and nilgai spoor and the ripple and flow of spots on the flanks of a leopard, to fan those embers into a steady flame. It was evident that deep in my heart I had already begun to hero-worship Corbett. As far as I was concerned, the man could do no wrong, as shikari, naturalist, writer or human being. It added immensely to the mystery and charisma of the man that he had hunted down—on a one-to-one basis as it were—ten man-eaters that had killed about 1000 human beings and terrorized large parts of Kumaon in the first four decades of the twentieth century. To my mind, no other hunter had written with such empathy about Indian wildlife, be it J. Forsyth, G.P. Sanderson, Dunbar Brander or those who followed, with the possible exception of R.A. Sterndale in *Seonee* and E.O. Shebbeare in *Soondar Moonee*. So tenacious was Corbett's grip on my imagination that it took no time at all for the mere interest to grow rapidly into an obsession. Each moment that I have spent during the next thirty-odd years in sojourns at the country's national parks and sanctuaries, has allowed me to re-live, albeit at several removes, some of the experiences that Corbett had described in his books.

During the years I roamed through Palamau, Bandhavgarh, Kanha, the Corbett National Park and elsewhere, the alarm calls of the chital, the langur, the kakar and the sambar and, on occasion, of peafowl and jungle fowl, gave warning, times without number, of 'stripes' or 'spots' on the prowl. The pug marks, their edges sometimes sharp and clear or blurred with the passage of time, imprinted in the soil near some nullah or waterhole, began to tell their own fascinating story. I developed a deeper understanding of the nuances of tone and volume as I listened to the strident call of the tiger in search of a mate and its savage snarls when disturbed at a kill or engaged in the act of mating.

With time, several unexpected questions about Corbett surfaced in my mind. Was it possible, I wondered, for a person to have known so much about the jungle? To have possessed the physical and mental powers of endurance to go without food for over sixty hours in pursuit of a man-eater? To have had the raw courage and enough confidence in his firearm to risk a shot at a man-eating tiger from a distance of no more than a few feet? What sort of a man was he? Were his extraordinary exploits in the forest real or make-believe? But then, there was too much documentary evidence in the man's favour to support such a conjecture.

ॐ

Corbett's birth centenary came and went in 1975 without making a splash. A few articles about him appeared in newspapers, and some meagre facts emerged about his birth in the last quarter of the nineteenth century in Nainital, in what was then the United Provinces. They also recorded that he had had business interests as well as hunting experiences in Africa, something Corbett had not mentioned either in *Jungle Lore* or in *My India* or, for that matter, in any of the rare autobiographical references in his other books. It seemed from some of the photographs accompanying the articles that Corbett had shot elephants, even in India. Again, there was no mention of this in any of his books. After that brief burst of newsworthiness, however, Corbett seemed to fade again from public memory.

But publishers, like film-makers, know a lode when they strike one and are adept at bringing out sequels. I was heartened when Oxford University Press (OUP), which had published Corbett's own writings, printed in 1978 R.E. Hawkins's *Jim Corbett's India*, an anthology focusing specifically on Corbett's writings on India, rather than on his hunts. Hawkins had edited most of Corbett's works including his first book, *Man-Eaters of Kumaon* (a title apparently preferred by the publishers to Corbett's own, more mundane, *Jungle Tales* to lend the stories more 'bite'). Hawkins had worked on this maiden venture of Corbett's in 1944, while he was with OUP in Mumbai. Hawkins's introduction to the book also revealed a number of hitherto unknown autobiographical details about Corbett that he himself had never mentioned in his writings. For the first time the reading public discovered, for instance, that Jim Corbett had been born in Nainital to Irish parents, Christopher William Corbett and Mary Jane Doyle (née Prussia) on 25 July 1875. Further details about Corbett's career in the railways, his tenure with the Nainital Municipal Board, his forays into East Africa and the setting up of the Corbett Museum at Kaladhungi also found mention. Hawkins's eleven-page introduction however failed to satisfy my ever-growing curiosity about the hunter and naturalist.

In 1979 came Kala's book, *Jim Corbett of Kumaon*, bursting with a wealth of fresh information on the hunter. The author, who is himself from Nainital, mentions in the preface that he had written the book for Corbett fans and that it was his way of accounting for the debt of gratitude he felt was owed to the hunter. For Corbett had not only done much to protect the people of Kumaon from the threat of man-eaters, he had also contributed significantly towards the conservation of wildlife. Kala was able to access considerable archival material from the municipality office and the church of St John-in-the-Wilderness and sift through other records available at Nainital, besides the valuable notes provided by Corbett's sister, Maggie, to Ruby Beyts, a friend and neighbour from their days in Kenya. Reading Kala's book was a far more satisfying experience for me, especially as it contained the author's perceptive observations and notes on Corbett as a person. This was followed in 1986 by Martin Booth's *Carpet Sahib*. Booth had been able to get in touch with a number of Corbett's relations, friends, colleagues, neighbours and well-wishers and retrieve, apart from some interesting photographs, more personal details about the hunter.

The urge to know more about Corbett the man and to see for myself the places where he had hunted and fished, took me to Nainital and Kaladhungi in November 1986. There I visited the Corbett Museum and explored the forests along the Boar (or is it the Baur, the name used by Kala?) river which had been a part of the hunter's beat more than half a century earlier. And it was during these peregrinations that my nearly feverish obsession with the hunter abated, only to be replaced by a more focussed interest in Corbett as a human being. It became important for me to know, for instance, how tall he was, to acquaint myself with the different facets of his personality including his foibles and idiosyncrasies that would peg him down to the level of mere mortals and bring him within my reach and understanding. I was keen to fathom the limits of his phenomenal powers of endurance and to determine the point at which knowledge and experience, as Corbett himself put it, overtook the primal fear of the jungle. The journey from a childhood adulation of Corbett the hunter to a more discerning perspective on Corbett the man was to take me more than fifteen years to complete.

A Measure of the Man

In 1985, laid up for over a month with a heart ailment, I rediscovered my childhood fascination for Corbett's books and read them from cover to cover more than once. What was more, propped up in bed, I faithfully followed the hunter's descriptions and took to sketching out in a drawing book the lay of the land in and around Kaladhungi and at the locations where Corbett had shot the man-eating tigers. It was a fascinating exercise to trace in the imagination and on the pages of the drawing book the twists and turns of the ravines and nullahs, to trek up hill and down dale, skirting the ridges and saddles of the Kumaon hills, accompanying Corbett, so to speak, as he tracked his man-eaters. Increasingly, these notes and sketches would lend greater immediacy to Corbett's writings and enable me to understand better the topography of the terrain and the nature of the jungles he had walked through and hunted in.

From Corbett's *Jungle Lore* (along with *My India*, this book contains whatever minor biographical references he has conceded) and his biographies by D.C.

Kala and Martin Booth I learnt that Jim's childhood had not been very different from that of other expatriate children of his time who were domiciled in India, particularly those who lived far away from the big towns and cantonments. In the days of the British Raj, Nainital had been the summer capital of the provincial government of what was then known as the United Provinces which sprawled across a large swathe of land along the foothills of the Himalaya, from Punjab in the west to Bihar in the east and extending into the plains between the Yamuna and the Ganga. In the hills of Kumaon and Garhwal, which are located here, lie a number of remnant glacial or spring-fed lakes. Nainital, discovered by the British in 1862, happens to be one of them. Legend has it that the goddess Nanda Devi had shed a tear on this very spot on her way to Mansarovar. It was from this teardrop that a lake—Nainital—had sprung. Like many other families then living in Nainital, the Corbetts were forced into an emergency evacuation when their house on the slopes of the northern ridge below Sher-ka-Danda came in the way of a major landslide caused by torrential rains on 15 September 1880. They had to set up house all over again in the Ayarpata area on the southern ridge. Unfortunately, Jim's father died a few months later. The responsibilities of the large family now fell on Tom, Jim's eldest brother, who had found a job with the postal department. It may have been during the same year, around November, that Jim came down with pneumonia. As he puts it, for a while it was touch and go with him as he hovered between life and death. What eventually pulled him through was the untiring care he received from his mother and sisters along with strong moral support from Tom who gave him a catapult with which he roamed the jungles around his house for the next couple of years.

Jim has given an illuminating account of this phase of his life in *Jungle Lore*. He describes how he had to escort the women in his family and from the neighbours' to the Boar canal for their bath and how, when he found himself alone during his first shoot with Tom on a hillside near their home in Kaladhungi, he had to keep his fear firmly in check as he watched a bear approach. Corbett also mentions his outing with one of their neighbours, Dansey, during which he used a firearm for the first time in his life and got knocked off his feet by the recoil of the gun. It was around this time that his cousin, Stephen Dease, lent Jim a muzzle-loader to collect bird specimens to illustrate a book that Dease was planning to write. And it is impossible to forget Corbett's description of his first sighting of a leopard as a young boy, while walking along the Nainital–Kaladhungi road with his dog, Magog. But the crowning glory of his experiences during his childhood was ten-year-old Jim's shooting of a leopard in the jungles behind Arundel, their old house in Kaladhungi. Needless to say, these events were instrumental in shaping Corbett's mind and attitude, as borne out by the later years of his life.

As mentioned earlier, the introductory notes by R.E. Hawkins in his book *Jim Corbett's India* (a copy of which I had received as a gift in 1981) contains the first references to Corbett the man by someone who had possibly met him on a couple of occasions. Hawkins had edited the manuscript of *Man-Eaters of Kumaon*, sent to him in 1943 and accompanied by glowing testimonials from Lord Linlithgow, then viceroy of India, and Sir Maurice Hallet, governor of the United Provinces at the time. Hawkins's notes and the books on Corbett by Kala and Booth that followed, filled an important gap in the information available on the hunter's life.

Strangely enough, instead of writing about his own impressions of Corbett in his book, Hawkins quotes Govind Ram Kala, a former civil servant who had been posted in Kumaon and had met the hunter quite a few times since the 1920s, describing him as a man of average height, with a swarthy complexion. D.C. Kala has mentioned elsewhere that Marjorie Clough, a nurse with the Red Cross who had met Corbett in India during World War II, described him to be about six feet tall with a ruddy complexion. That was enough to set me off on a sort of wild 'height' chase that seems to have run out of steam only recently.

Corbett's photographs tell us that he took after his father—with a pug nose, a high forehead, rather prominent cheekbones, firm chin and deep-set eyes. His was a decidedly 'expatriate' face, as we Indians know it. If one goes by the pictures taken of Corbett in his youth and during World War I, he was not bad-looking either. Beyond these details lies the grey area of conjecture. Kala brings up a comment by Geoffrey Cumberledge (who had met the hunter several times and was the publisher for OUP when Corbett's first books were under way) that Corbett was tall and spare with dark brown hair and light blue eyes. In a letter he wrote to me, Booth (who had done a good deal of research for his biography of Corbett) states, however, that the hunter was just over six feet tall and had mousy-brown hair and brown eyes. So we have two different colours for Corbett's eyes from two separate sources!

At least, Cumberledge and Booth agree that the hunter was fairly tall, which is more than can be said for the conflicting observations of others. One of the villagers I met at Kaladhungi claimed to have seen Corbett in the early 1940s. He was very confident in his assertion that the hunter had been around five feet eight inches in height. On the other hand, two residents of Nainital who had also met Corbett around the same time, claimed that the hunter was about five feet ten inches tall. Both his parents were short; so was his sister, Maggie. Therefore, one may not be too wrong in assuming that Corbett had been between five foot nine and five foot ten, depending on whether one measured him between nose and tail, or over the curves—methods normally used for 'sizing up' dead tigers! Somehow, this exercise, aimed at visualizing Corbett's physical features in an attempt to penetrate the wall of reserve with which he had surrounded himself, afforded me a kind of vicarious pleasure.

As for his weight, from what Corbett mentions in the chapter on Sultana in *My India* he was about fifty-seven kilograms lighter than Freddy Young, an officer of the Imperial Police Force posted in the United

Provinces, who weighed around 127 kilograms. That would make Corbett's weight around seventy kilograms. If photographs are anything to go by and we are to take into consideration several descriptions of his loping gait, then Corbett's build can be characterized as rangy.

In a bid to get my growing hunger for information about every aspect of Corbett's life out of my system, I began to put my thoughts down on paper. In an article I wrote for the *Telegraph*, Calcutta, published in its Sunday supplement on 21 August 1986, I rued the way biographical details about the hunter had either been deliberately suppressed or were scattered about in a haphazard manner in personal correspondence and in sections of his various books. I could not help confessing at the same time that to pursue Corbett's trail by following up the most tenuous of leads could be a fascinating exercise. My own view of the hunter as a person, based on the impressions that had emerged from his writings, was, 'a reserved—even taciturn—person, capable of superhuman effort and perseverance, innately public-spirited, awkward in public view, but capable of deep and abiding relationships with a select few'.

It seemed intriguing that although Corbett had had his grounding in jungle lore in the forests in and around Kaladhungi in the terai area, he hunted for man-eaters at relatively higher altitudes in Champawat, Mukteswar (he refers to the place as 'Muktesar') and Talla Des.

It is rather mystifying, even exasperating, that Corbett had been so reticent about the details regarding when and where he had shot the man-eaters. Some dates he mentions, others he omits. Even his books do not cover his hunts in a systematic manner. Nor do they follow a chronological order. Corbett goes forward, then turns back in time. There was, apparently, a lull between 1910, when he shot the Mukteswar man-eater, and 1926, when the man-eater of Rudraprayag met its untimely end at his hands. By the time Corbett had shot the 'Bachelor' of Powalgarh (in 1930), he was already fifty-five years old. A lesser man would have settled for the safety and comforts of retirement. Not so Corbett, who subsequently undertook two of his most arduous and dangerous hunts—one for the Chowgarh tigers in April 1930, the other for the Thak man-eater in November 1938—when he was sixty-three years old! Not content to call it a day, Jim also developed a new passion: wildlife photography, which he pursued with zeal with his 16-mm camera. Several of the wildlife films he shot are preserved in the archives of the British Museum of Natural History in London.

Little did I realize that far from satiating my interest in Corbett the little bit of research I had done on him before writing the article would merely whet my appetite for further insights into a man who reveals himself only fleetingly in the pages of his books, much as the tigers he hunted moved invisibly from cover to cover, there but not quite there, like a will-o'-the-wisp.

First Foot Forward

It was one thing to convalesce in Calcutta, where I live, and sketch the terrain and routes that Corbett had described in his books, and quite another to acquire first-hand knowledge of Kaladhungi, Nainital and the jungles of Kumaon that lay more than 1500 kilometres away. The rhododendron, oak, chestnut, pine and deodar forests that Corbett had written of were a far cry from the sal, simul, palas and bamboo of Palamau and Bandhavgarh's dry deciduous forests with which I had become relatively more familiar by the 1980s.

The urge to move out of the confines of the sketchbook to the jungles of Kumaon nearly forty years after Corbett had written about them was so powerful that one chilly morning in November 1986 saw me stepping off the Nainital Express at Haldwani. Eighteen years ago, this used to be just a small town, almost a way station for the better-known hill resort of Nainital. Except for the main road that ran from Bareilly past Haldwani and Kathgodam to Nainital, most thoroughfares were either not metalled or so poorly maintained that they resembled rocky village paths.

There were hardly any cars to be seen; horse and mule-drawn carriages and carts, along with cycle rickshaws, reigned supreme. Even the metre-gauge railway line, the low station platform and the small rail coaches were a throwback to a gentler past, distinct from the busy broad-gauge rail line that now goes past Haldwani up to Kathgodam. Beyond the railway tracks, a deep bluish-green blanket of forest stretched across the low foothills of Kumaon and looked mysteriously inviting. As I alighted from the train, I shivered slightly, as much from the early morning chill as with the anticipation of getting closer to my quarry.

Up along the ghat road past Ranibag and Jeolikot, Nainital in 1986 was itself a far cry from the well-developed and much-frequented resort town it has now become. A handful of hotels, mostly of questionable standard, dotted Tallital, the south-eastern end of the lake, while a few, including the tourist lodge, were perched on a ridge in the Sukhatal area overlooking Mallital and the Naina Devi temple at the south-western end. The lake itself is cradled between two long, high ridges that run immediately to the north and south of it in an almost east–west direction. The road from Haldwani pops up over a saddle and before you know it the bus has taken a sharp turn and there lies the lake, gleaming in the sunlight. There is something infinitely special about an emerald-green lake nestling in densely wooded hills, with the sunlight glancing off the water's surface and illuminating one portion of it and then another, before casting shadows and moving on as the day wanes. You tend to overlook the rash of human dwellings and the din and clatter emanating from shops and restaurants nearby, as you stroll lazily down the sun-dappled Mall that runs along the northern edge of the lake to the municipal office and the Naina Devi temple, perched slightly further up, the entire path flanked by poplar, oak and chestnut trees. The lake's southern shore, usually always in the shadow of the ridge, is so chilly that it makes you want to hurry down the 'Thandi Sarak', if you can persuade yourself at all to go walking there. In the Nainital of yore, cars were few and far between and you generally walked or, if you were a tourist, rode up to or along the ridges on horseback.

My inquiries about some of the places with which Corbett had been associated, such as his first school on Sher-ka-Danda, high up on the north ridge, Gurney House, where the hunter and his family lived for more than half a century before Maggie and Jim left for Kenya in 1947, and the church of St John-in-the-Wilderness, drew blank stares from the *paanwallah* and the hotel waiter. The Naina Devi temple, mentioned more than once by Corbett in his books (although he refers to it as the temple of Nanda Devi, the goddess of the great snow-clad mountain in the Kumaon Himalaya) was, therefore, the first place I visited. Visible across the lake, the temple is situated on its south-west shore, near the Capitol cinema, a newly constructed gurdwara and the round bandstand at the water's edge that was built with a donation from Corbett. Dedicated to a hill goddess beloved of the locals, the Naina Devi temple is compact, double-storeyed and unostentatious, with an open veranda in front, a gabled roof and a tapering red spire. A chain of brass bells in different sizes hangs across the entrance. They have been strung up by devotees who strike them everytime they enter the premises. I noticed that the prayers chanted by the devotees were generally brief, rounded off with the observance of a ritual such as a symbolic scattering of flowers, the tying of a garland or, at best, the splitting of a coconut on the threshold of the inner sanctum. In acknowledgement of the pilgrim's devotion and to mark his visit, the priest smeared the forehead of each visitor with the typical ochre and red tika and a few grains of rice. Corbett writes that it was near this temple by the lake that he had buried the fingers of the woman who was the last victim of the Champawat tiger, an animal with the dubious distinction of having been the first man-eater the hunter had bagged way back in 1907. The temple priest whom Corbett had known must have passed on. The current incumbent knew nothing about the hunter and seemed less interested in my queries about him than in the fresh batch of devotees arriving at the temple.

Standing in the temple compound, with the waters of the lake lapping at my feet, I tried to visualize Nainital as it used to be almost seventy years ago. Then, the lake had been larger. More than one landslide and the denudation of forest cover resulting in progressive soil erosion had brought earth and rocks crashing down to the water's edge. Waste and sludge, the bane of a growing population, had also taken their inevitable toll over the years. Corbett has written that in his time the forests near and around the town were inhabited by kakar, bears and leopards. In fact, Olive Smythies, wife of E.A. Smythies, a forest officer posted in Kumaon, mentions in her book, *Tiger Lady*, that in the early years of the twentieth century, tigers, including a man-eater, had been frequenting Kilbury, no more than seven kilometres from Nainital. A comparison of old photographs of the town and recent ones clearly shows up the adverse effects of the construction boom, with buildings crowding closer to the Mall on the sunny northern side of the lake. Equally apparent are the increasingly bare patches of soil, devoid of tree cover, higher up on the hillside.

Development along the flanks of the south ridge, which lies mostly in shadow above the Thandi Sarak, seemed to have been relatively less hurried. Several of the older houses dating back to the beginning of the twentieth century had survived and coexisted with more recent structures. A walk down the Thandi Sarak takes one past the Hanuman temple. This house of worship, along with the one dedicated to Pashani Devi, where Corbett had occasionally dropped by to chat with the priests and, according to some, even to offer prayers, was still active and regularly frequented by devotees. Here, the traditional Kumaoni idols in bas-relief, gleaming with the oil and ochre lovingly smeared on them by generations of worshippers, rested under a canopy of tall trees, surrounded by a scattering of oak and chestnut. Close by, right at the water's edge and now surrounded by a low railing, lay the large rock near which Corbett had caught a mahseer weighing about twenty-three kilograms. Kala's book has a photograph of this trophy, and an enlarged version of the same picture is on display at the Corbett Museum in Kaladhungi.

If the face of the north ridge is the place for hotels and resorts, the south ridge serves as the location for the town's many well-known schools—Sherwood, St Paul's, All Saints, St Joseph's and St Mary's. It is not clear from available records whether Corbett had ever studied at any of these schools. According to one report, however, he had begun his formal education when he was eight years old at the Philander Smith School (now the Birla School) situated at Sher-ka-Danda. Corbett reportedly continued his studies at the Diocesan Boys' School which, according to Booth and others, has metamorphosed into the present-day Sherwood College, located on the south ridge overlooking the town. In notes dictated by Maggie to Ruby Beyts, she remembers her brother as an indifferent student but an avid reader, especially of books by James Fenimore Cooper such as *The Pathfinders*, *The Deerhunter* and *The Last of the Mohicans*. These romanticized tales of adventure must have encouraged young Jim to fantasize and trek barefoot through the jungles, acting out with bow and arrow the role of the hunter he was destined to become one day.

A little further to the west along the south ridge, lower down the slope near Ayarpata, stands Gurney House. The first time I went up there in 1986, it was on pony-back—the climb from the 'Flats' at Mallital to the house, all the way up the steep hillside, had been quite beyond my plains-bred lungs. I remember how the old muleteer had led his charge, the pony's hooves slipping and slithering on the paved pathway that twisted its way around the houses, climbing higher and higher, while I clung precariously to the saddle. More than midway up the Ayarpata ridge, where the road banked to the left, stood the old Corbett home, enclosed within a fairly large compound dotted with oak, chestnut and deodar trees. The house, which stood on the south face of the north ridge, had come up after Jim's father had passed away and the infamous earthquake of September 1880 had shaken Nainital, forcing the Corbetts to abandon their old home. Gurney House had been built around 1882 and some of the timber and materials from the old Corbett home had reportedly been used in its construction.

The house looked its age. A long wooden veranda, sheltered under a gabled roof of corrugated tin, ran for about twelve metres or so along the north face of the building overlooking Mallital. At the eastern end the veranda turned around the large bay window of the drawing room. The kitchen lay to the west of the veranda, while the bedrooms, located along the south face, overlooked a relatively flat portion of the hillside. The western end of the compound contained the outhouses once inhabited by the domestic help. Disappointed that the house was locked, I spent some time strolling around the compound, taking a couple of pictures as keepsakes. It was a way of trying to get a feel of the place where Corbett had lived for the better part of his life. As far as I could see, it was still green all around, with a number of tall trees throwing much of the house and compound into shadow. With more houses coming up in the neighbourhood and trees becoming scarcer, the environment must have changed considerably since Corbett's time. Just standing before the bay window where Jim and Maggie must have sat so many times, sipping tea, and walking down the same path, traced and retraced by their footsteps as they went past the same deodar and chestnut trees, gave me an indescribable thrill and a deep sense of satisfaction.

The next day I took a bus that followed a route hugging the south-western part of the ridge above Nainital, past Sukhatal and Khurpatal, along the ghat road that led from the hill station down to the plains. Times without number, Corbett had walked down this road between Kaladhungi and Nainital to attend to official or personal work. Of course, the landmarks along the route have changed somewhat over the last 100 years or so. The upper reaches have little tree cover and particularly jagged cliffs and rocks. The slopes were given over, then as now, to terrace cultivation. Narrow, arching fields buttressed on the slopes with a fringe of rocks to prevent the soil from being carried down during the rains had been carved out of the hillside by back-breaking human labour. It was along this road zigzagging through the scrub jungle that an eight-year-old Jim, out on a stroll with his dog, had sighted a leopard for the first time when it had leapt down the hillside on being disturbed by some milkmen. Past Khurpatal, however, trees made a welcome reappearance and by the time we were nearing the junction, where this road joins the one that runs between Haldwani and Ramnagar, the forest was thick with an abundance of sal trees. It was along the lower stretch of this road that the bearskin episode (mentioned in *Jungle Lore*) involving Dansey and Neil Fleming, with Corbett as an unwitting accomplice, had taken place.

Directly across from the point where I had stepped off the bus at the junction, a small signboard drew my attention to the Corbett Museum. I was in Kaladhungi or rather Chhota Haldwani village (although Corbett himself never used this name to refer to it in his books). The Kaladhungi bazaar lay some two kilometres to the east. It was here, by the Boar, that Corbett's father had been granted residential land in 1869 by Sir Henry Ramsay. It was here that the hunter had been initiated into the ways of the jungle and had spent his later years with Maggie. In 1986, the jungle extended a short distance at both ends beyond Kaladhungi and lay partly to the north of the road, while to the south lay expanses of cultivated land. The dense jungles of the terai, near and around the villages mentioned by Corbett (such as Nayagaon and Garuppu) and the grasslands or maidan near Bajpur and Rudrapur had largely surrendered to the plough. Some patches of forest still persisted near and around Garuppu. Significant, however, are Corbett's own observations in *Jungle Lore* about the considerable changes he had witnessed in his lifetime in the bhabar and terai region. Where there had been grassland, forests had come up and a secondary growth of scrubs had replaced what had once been dense forest. In fact, some of the hills contained iron ore and, as mentioned by Corbett in *My India*, iron was smelted at Kaladhungi with wood charcoal being used as fuel and reductant. Apprehending a serious depletion of the local forests, Sir Henry Ramsay, then superintendent of the terai region, had ordered these ironworks shut down by the last quarter of the nineteenth century.

Little known to most Indians, the Jim Corbett Museum is a small memorial to the hunter set up in the 1970s by an enterprising officer of the Uttar Pradesh forest department. Housed in the two small bungalows that the Corbett family had used as their winter home in Kaladhungi, the museum stands directly opposite the point where the new Public Works Department (PWD) road from Nainital joins the road now linking Haldwani to Ramnagar. The road with its new landmarks runs for about thirty-four kilometres from Nainital. Older residents of Kaladhungi remember a shorter District Board road (or *ghoria* road, fit for travelling on horseback) that ran for twenty-two kilometres or so from the hill station. The Corbett house stands a couple of kilometres from Kaladhungi bazaar, which in turn lies about twenty-five kilometres from Haldwani, the railhead for visitors to Nainital. The Corbett Museum stands on roughly four acres of land, about 100 metres east of the Boar. An iron gate with a huge old kanju (*Holoptelea integrifolia*) tree beside it is set into its stone boundary wall. There are several mango trees on the property, and a toon (*Cedrela toona*) and a haldu (*Adina cordifolia*) tree stand sentinel along the front wall. The museum houses quite a collection of Corbett memorabilia, all carefully labelled and described accurately and in detail.

Here and there in his books, especially in *Jungle Lore*, Corbett has given vivid descriptions of Kaladhungi as it used to be during his lifetime—the Boar, the canal which sluiced off water from the river to the village, the watercourses that flowed down to his ancestral house, the road to Kotabag and Powalgarh that ran up the right bank of the river across the bridge straddling the river, the cane thickets at Dhunigar, near Nayagaon village, nearly five kilometres away, the mixed jungle, typical of the transition zone between the bhabar and the terai, full of plum (ber, *Zisyphus jujuba*) bushes and khair (*Acacia catechu*), runi (*Mallotus phillipensis*), simul (*Bombax malabaricum*), haldu, pipal (*Ficus religiosa*), kusum (*Schleichera oleosa*) and sisam (*Dalbergia sissoo*) trees, the glades and grasslands, primarily of nal (*Phragmites karka*), the stretches of sal forest and, of course, oak and chestnut trees and rhododendron bushes at higher elevations. In the opposite direction towards Haldwani, and around twenty-nine kilometres to the west, lies Ramnagar. Corbett passed through here on his way to Garjia (not 'Gargia', as he spelt it) and Mohan, from where Moradabad and Rampur could also be accessed. About four kilometres down the road to Ramnagar lies Nayagaon; Garuppu and Rudrapur are fifteen and forty kilometres away respectively, down a subsidiary road that runs south. A road runs across the Boar and slices through fairly dense forest and across the shoulder of a hill towards Kotabag and Powalgarh.

Hardy agriculturalists from West Punjab and a

number of artisans and farmers from East Bengal had settled in the area following the Partition of the country in 1947. It is said that Corbett fell out with the late Govind Ballabh Pant, then chief minister of Uttar Pradesh, over the possible repercussions of such resettlement. For Corbett, the very thought of the jungles being cleared, his beloved terai put to the plough and the deer, pig and tiger that lived there shot to extinction or driven out of their natural habitat must have been unbearable. When I visited the area, the growth in human population over forty years since 1947 had also taken its toll. Some 'sainik farms' which provided supplies to the army had, moreover, been set up. A few areas had been planted with eucalyptus and poplar, changing, irrevocably, the vista of dense natural jungle that lay to the north of the Haldwani–Ramnagar road.

When I stepped off the bus at this junction, I noticed that there was hardly a handful of houses in the area. Across the road, encircling the compound in which stood the two cottages where Jim had lived with his mother and his two sisters, Mary Doyle and Maggie, was the low wall of rocks the hunter had erected in the 1920s to keep out deer and pigs. Was it on one of the haldu trees nearby that Corbett had seen, shortly after the 'Kaiser's War', what he alluded to as the *churail* in *Jungle Lore*? He described it as a bird, slightly smaller than an eagle, with fairly long legs, a neck that was neither too long nor too short and a head that was quite unlike the owl's round one. Having gone through the compact edition of *The Handbook of Birds of India and Pakistan* by Salim Ali and S. Dillon Ripley, I felt that this may well have been the Crested Hawk Eagle (*Spizaetus limnaeetus*) which is slightly over half a metre long (as opposed to the size of the Golden Eagle which is nearly a metre in length), has fairly long legs and is usually not found north of Etawah in south-central Uttar Pradesh (hence Corbett's claim of not having come across the bird in the Kumaon jungles). Its call has been described in the *Handbook* as ending in a long-drawn-out scream, while its nocturnal cries resemble the wail of a woman being strangled. Thus the superstitious village folk of the area may well have mistaken the call of this bird for the cry of the *churail*, an evil spirit in female form.

The Corbett compound was relatively small, covering less than four acres. Far from the bustling tourist spot it had become when I visited it about fifteen years later, complete with a public telephone booth, shops selling potato wafers, mineral water and aerated drinks, Kaladhungi in 1986 still seemed a sleepy place, its residents content with eking out a living of sorts in the shadow of the hills and forests. The cottages were part of the 'New House' that had been acquired by the Uttar Pradesh forest department in 1965, apparently from Chiranjilal Shah, a former manager of the Nainital Bank and an acquaintance of Corbett's. The house had been the subject of some correspondence between Corbett and Shah because the former had wanted to hand it over to be used as the office of the village panchayat. As I entered through the gate leading into the compound and moved straight ahead, I came face to face with Corbett's bust. To the right, very close to the compound wall lies Robin's grave. An English springer spaniel (apparent from his photographs and confirmed as such by Corbett in *Jungle Lore*), Robin had been acquired as a puny pup from the 'Knight of the Broom', as the hunter jocularly called the sweeper. The dog had accompanied Corbett on many a hunt, including the one for the man-eating 'Bachelor' of Powalgarh in 1930. Alluding, over a decade later, to Robin's death, Corbett falls back on the poetic licence to which all writers stake a claim and states that his pet had moved on to the 'happy hunting grounds' while lying at his feet, even as his master was busy writing. It seems more likely that Robin—who seems to have been around four years old in 1930—died sometime in the late 1930s when Corbett was away in East Africa.

The larger bungalow to the west was a far cry from the elegant residences that can be seen in some Indian hill stations, including Nainital. Modest in size, almost diminutive, with hardly eight metres of veranda in front, it was supported by four pillars and topped by a shallow, gabled roof. Access to the bungalow lay through a long room. It led to two rather small rooms and a somewhat larger drawing room with a little fireplace along its western wall. A narrow landing connected the building to a still smaller cottage, comprising just one room, a toilet and a tiny veranda, hardly four and a half metres long. This was where Corbett preferred to live, although he often slept in a small tent set up in the compound. It was a habit inspired, perhaps, by his friend and mentor, Sir Percy Wyndham, a former commissioner of

Kumaon, who was often out on tour for official work and had gone on record with the remark that he mostly spent Christmas under canvas!

The larger bungalow has been converted into a museum dedicated to Corbett memorabilia. This consists of some of his furniture, including a cane settee, and a few articles he is said to have used, like his 'shooting' lamp, which the hunter does not mention in his books and which, in all likelihood, he used while out camping or during night-fishing stints at Nainital and Bhimtal. Among the exhibits are pieces of crockery, including an outsized teacup that Corbett had apparently drunk out of, a jungle hat made from felt (which Corbett had supposedly worn during his training of troops for the Burma campaign during World War II, for he generally wore a sola topee) and a *dandi*, a canvas seat suspended from two poles, which is said to have served as a kind of sedan chair for Maggie when she travelled to and from Nainital.

Also on display in glass cases are photographs of Corbett at different stages of his life—as a young man, as an officer during World War I and as a hunter getting on in years. In fact, there are several pictures of Corbett during or after a hunt, including the ones with the 'Bachelor' of Powalgarh and the fish weighing twenty-three kilograms which he had caught at Nainital. There are a few enlarged photocopies of Corbett's correspondence with his friends and acquaintances, penned in his curious, rounded script. The smaller cottage houses a couple of cane chairs, an upright gunrack-cum-case, a few well-worn walking sticks and, in the bathroom, a large earthenware jar, less than a metre high and almost as broad, obviously used for storing water for a bath. The customary thunderbox was, however, nowhere in sight.

I managed to get hold of one of the forest guards entrusted with the care of the premises and somehow persuaded him to show me around. The Boar runs from north to south less than a 100 metres west of the bungalows. Although it is between thirty and forty metres wide, the river lacks the depth and force that had once brought shoals of mahseer within reach of Corbett's fish-hook. This might be due to the construction, a few kilometres upstream, of a fairly large reservoir which feeds the canals in the area. Its banks overgrown with secondary forests on either side and the bed raised a great deal by boulders brought down from the hills, the Boar seemed to be a different river from the one Corbett had described in his books. Of course, the single-span steel bridge which had replaced the wooden cantilevered one used during Corbett's own lifetime, was still in position, and rattled and shook as buses and other heavy vehicles thundered over it. The forest guard and I walked across the bridge and went a short distance up the forest road that takes off to the right, along the right bank of the Boar, towards Kotabag, fourteen kilometres away. From there, Powalgarh is another seven kilometres.

The guard led me diagonally across from the two cottages to a large compound that spread over nearly twelve acres of land. Overlooking it was a dilapidated house, standing on a high plinth. Locally known as the *khandar* or ruins, it was occupied by a milkman who owned a couple of milch cows and buffaloes. Recalling the sketches I had seen in one of the earlier editions of the hunter's books, I was able to identify the ruins as Arundel, the ancestral home of the Corbetts, where the family had lived for over twenty years since 1869. The plan of the house was rather curious: it had a large, south-facing front room, about 6 metres by 9 metres, with an open veranda overlooking the Haldwani–Ramnagar road. A fireplace positioned in the centre of its northern wall was flanked by doors on either side leading to two rooms, each measuring around 3 metres by 3.7 metres. Beyond them lay four more rooms, measuring about 2 metres by 2.4 metres each. I wondered whether these were indeed the rooms where the seven Corbett siblings had slept. Some distance from the main residence stood the cookhouse. The compound contained a handful of old simul trees and two large haldu trees to the north, where a canal flowed down from the Boar.

What really excited me, though, were the large elephant footprints in the compound. A herd had apparently visited the area during the previous monsoon. There was little doubt in my mind that the hunter had come across elephants near Kanda and in the Kosi valley near Mohan, where he had shot the two man-eaters named after these places in his accounts, for I saw them fifty years later when I visited Corbett National Park. It was also quite likely that Jim had sighted elephants near Tanakpur and along the Nandhour; they were very much there when I visited the area seventy years later. Corbett does not mention them, however, except in *Jungle Lore*, where he gives an enthralling account of a fight between a tusker and a pair of tigers, reported near Tanakpur in the early years of the twentieth century. Pausing under the simul trees which stood along the western edge of the compound surrounding Arundel, I tried to visualize what it must have been like almost a century earlier, during Corbett's childhood, with the jungle encroaching on the edge of the canal, the calls of chital, kakar and peafowl resounding in the thickets nearby and the occasional roar of a tiger chilling the blood, as it returned to its lair in the neighbouring hills after feeding contentedly on a kill.

By this time the sun was dipping in the west. We walked down the bank of the canal to the point where a small stone bridge crossed it, before returning along a path on the other side. In a short while, we came upon the first of the watercourses running down from the hills and mentioned time and again in Corbett's books. The water of the canal was carried down by an aqueduct, in all likelihood the Bijli Dant referred to in *Jungle Lore*. All around was fairly thick mixed forest. It required little imagination to understand why Corbett would never venture into the forests nearby during his childhood without first checking the sandy bed of the watercourse for pug marks. It was his way of ensuring that no tiger had crossed it to lurk in the thickets just ahead. A cattle track lay across the watercourse. We could hear the cackling of jungle fowl as they made one last effort to collect their dinner before calling it a day. We made our way to the second watercourse, which lay about 100 metres further on. Little boys were driving their cattle home in the gentle light of the setting sun. Women passed us, bundles of firewood balanced on their heads. It seemed as though a scene from *Jungle Lore* were being acted out before our very eyes.

I managed dinner with a plate of chapattis and vegetables coaxed out of the forest guard, and spent the night on a cot set up on the kitchen veranda along the south wall, some distance from the cottages. There were no visitations from the 'other' world as far as I could make out and the night passed without incident, disturbed just by a round of alarm calls from a barking deer, perhaps from the Nainital road a kilometre away.

The morning was greeted by a babel of calls from the early birds, especially jungle fowl and the hair-crested drongo. After sharing tea and biscuits, the forest guard and I went for a walk up the road to Nainital (those were the days, unencumbered by the visitors' register and the entrance coupon that would become mandatory from 2001 for tourists visiting the Corbett Museum). A short distance up the road, to the left, stood the forest rest house where, more•than once, Corbett had had differences of opinion with visiting shikaris about the shooting of leopards and tigers in the area. Huge haldu trees cast their shade over the rest house which stood on a metre-high plinth, facing the east. A wide veranda, spaced at regular intervals with pillars and shaded by venetian blinds, ran along its front. Behind the bungalow and to the west flowed the Boar. To the right of the road, a stone bridge spanned the canal, the same bridge which the Pipal Pani tiger had limped over some fifty years ago. On either side of the road, regenerated sal thickets obscured the view. Only the narrow strip of road, ribboning out of the folds of the hill on the river's left bank, stretched before us.

We left the road and entered the forest on our left through a game track. Soon enough, we came across relatively fresh hoof marks of kakar and sambar and, a little farther on, the pug marks of a leopard. Was it the one the kakar had been barking at the previous night, I wondered. All around us, the brown fissured trunks of sal rose like pillars. High up, the canopy of foliage reverberated with calls of drongos, minivets and nuthatches. The brilliant crimson of a yellow-backed sunbird flashed repeatedly like a beacon over our heads as it flitted about in search of food. We went down the slope to the river and walked over the boulders to the opposite bank. About 100 metres upstream from where we were crossing, a kakar gingerly made its way over the boulders, too engrossed in nibbling at the blades of grass that grew between them to take any notice of us.

The forest and the canal had witnessed and endured much over the nearly 100 years they had been around. They had watched in silence as the Corbett children bathed in the canal's waters, Jim running barefoot along the banks and down the watercourse, and the horned owl, that was frequently the target of the boys' catapults, flying off beyond reach. As I contemplated the scene, a feeling of warmth stole over me at the thought that I was witnessing, first-hand, what I had only read about earlier in books. I have to confess that whatever may have been the degree of satisfaction I derived from poring over Corbett's accounts of his days spent here, it could never quite match the excitement of my direct encounter with the area he had known so intimately, or the overwhelming sense of fulfilment I experienced at seeing it all with my own eyes.

Going Wild

I returned to Kaladhungi in November the following year after an abortive angling excursion to Bhimtal—it was too cold, the locals had said—where Corbett had fished and had, apparently, owned a small hunting-cum-fishing lodge. Bhimtal has not quite made it as a tourist attraction the way Nainital has, despite its tranquil scenic beauty. The reason could be its surrounding hills whose lower altitudes fail to offer the grand vista that Nainital does.

A couple of local tourists who had joined me at Bhimtal were keen to explore the Corbett Museum at Kaladhungi. They had a car, and we drove down in it via Nainital. This gave me another opportunity to take the Sukhatal–Khurpatal route down to the plains. While my companions explored the museum, my attention was diverted by the huge kanju tree that grew just by the iron gate leading into the compound. Something about the formation of the trunk and roots seemed to jog my memory and I took a picture of it. Returning home a few days later, I compared the photograph with the one I had seen in *Man-Eaters of Kumaon* which shows Jim posing with the dead 'Bachelor' of Powalgarh at his feet. It was quite clear that the original photograph had been taken at the foot of the same kanju tree. Here then was a tree that had survived the vicissitudes of over fifty years, from 1930, when the 'Bachelor' was shot, to 1987, when I had photographed it. As apparent in the old photograph, the tree was already mature in 1930, and it was still there when I visited the place a second time in 2002! I would not have been surprised at all to learn that it was at least a hundred years old.

We drove down to Ramnagar and managed to get accommodation in the forest rest house at Garjia, about seven kilometres from the town. The road ran along the right or west bank of the Kosi and cut across the folds of some low hills, while an almost vertical escarpment ran along the far side of the river. Corbett had trekked this way in 1932 when he was pursuing the Kanda man-eater and again in 1933 when he was tracking the Mohan man-eater. He had stayed at Garjia. It was here that he had heard (as he records in his story about the Mohan man-eater) the strange croaking of the frogs on the banks of the Kosi that resembled the sound of two stones being struck together with great force. Even in 1987 it was clear that the short distance between Ramnagar and Garjia had once been densely forested. The night I spent there was uneventful, except for the alarm call of sambar from the jungles behind the rest house, a heartening sign that wildlife had not disappeared altogether from the area.

Early next morning, we made a short foray into the Sitabani jungles that lay opposite the rest house. The track runs along a small stream that probably flows into the Kosi. The forest was dense with vegetation and huge trees stood close together on either side of the trail, their overhanging branches, intertwined with liana, meeting overhead. The birds were out in strength: bulbuls, drongos, minivets and nuthatches called incessantly from the branches overhead as they flitted about in search of tasty morsels. But the mammals put up a poor show: all we managed to spot was a kakar, though it is quite possible, of course, that several animals were watching us without our being aware of it!

We took the main road towards Mohan, right up to the spot where the temple of Garjia Devi stands on a rocky island in the middle of the Kosi. The temple is accessible across a causeway and we went over to pay our homage to its presiding deity. In November, the level of the river was low and we encountered no difficulties at all in crossing it, but one can well imagine the problems that pilgrims face when the river is in full spate during and immediately after the monsoon. With the onset of winter, some shepherds had come down from the hills of Ranikhet and beyond with their pack ponies. Gazing at the stout hill ponies with bags and panniers of goods slung over their backs, the herds of sheep with their thick winter coats, the black-and-tan sheepdogs which kept the flocks together and the hardy shepherds wrapped in thick shawls, we were transported right back to the 1920s and 1930s, when Corbett had passed through the region on his way to shoot the man-eating leopard of Rudraprayag and, later, the Mohan man-eater.

Shortly afterwards, we reached the Dhangarhi gate through which we entered the Corbett National Park. The park extends west of the road for about fifty kilometres, skirting the valley of the Ramganga, which swoops down from the hills further to the north. Corbett had been closely involved with the preservation of this area, where he had occasionally shot and fished. Together with the forest officer E.A. Smythies, Corbett had worked on the details of the sanctuary way back in the early 1930s and it had been formally constituted in 1935 as India's first national park. The park had originally been named after Sir Malcolm Hailey, then governor of what was known as the United Provinces, and had been appropriately renamed after Corbett in 1957. It was here that Project Tiger had been formally launched in 1973 by the Government of India to protect the Indian tiger.

The national park is a typical bhabar forest. Vast sal forests stretch across the high ground above the river, while a heavy cover of mixed forest, mainly of the moist deciduous kind, clothes the hill slopes. Dense thickets of grass grow on the *chaurs* (sandbanks) and numerous streams ripple through the mass of hills before flowing down to the Ramganga. The river and its feeder streams run past shingle banks and over boulders and gravel, quite unlike the sand and silt that line riverbeds at lower elevations in the terai, some distance from the hills. The Ramganga is the archetypal submontane river, along with the Kosi, the Boar, the Goula, the Nandhour, the Ladhya and the Sarda, where Corbett loved to fish. It was on the banks of the Ramganga that Corbett had more than once, come across the python, a reptile for which he reserved both a healthy respect and a strong aversion, as my own encounter with one of the creatures near Gathia Rau on the river was to remind me.

Fortunately we had reserved a room at the Sultan bungalow. Jim has commented on more than one occasion on the harassment he occasionally had to put up with from the 'red tape brigade'—his way of commenting on the rigid official procedures that were a part of the system—because he had occupied rooms in official bungalows without prior reservations, thus exposing the caretaker to censure or even dismissal. The Sultan bungalow lies in a shallow bowl encircled by sal groves with low hills all around. Unlike Corbett, who preferred his eighteen-kilogram tent to the relative comfort of the rest houses while he tracked tigers, and quite unequipped with either firearms or experience of the jungle, we were only too happy to make ourselves at home in the bungalow. The chowkidar hurried through his preparation of an early dinner with the rations we had brought. The reason for such haste was fairly obvious: the cookhouse stood some forty-five metres from the bungalow and the chowkidar was evidently shy of close encounters of the wild kind in an area where tigers and elephants were known to be fond of late evening visits. In point of fact, that very night we were startled awake by the frenzied banging of pots and pans and the low rumbles that indicate the presence of an elephant or an entire herd in the vicinity. It seemed that the chowkidar's anxiety had been well-founded, for the next morning we saw the huge footprints of an elephant on the wet ground near the handpump next to the cookhouse. The elephant had even bent the tin sheets of the cookhouse in an effort to force its trunk in to taste the leftovers from our dinner—a huge compliment, obviously, to the chowkidar, though he didn't regard the situation in quite the same light!

After an early breakfast, we followed the local forester who agreed to lead the way along one of the trails that went off at a tangent from the site of the bungalow. Although we came across the footprints of our nocturnal visitor to the bungalow—the hungry elephant—and the pug marks of a leopard further along the track, neither of the animals honoured us with an appearance. This was just as well because my friends from Bhimtal were quite new to the ways of the jungle and had we suddenly come upon a wild beast our companion, the forester, would have had quite a situation on his hands!

We left for Dhikala shortly afterwards, crossing on the way several streams and stretches of forest, rich with sal trees and mixed vegetation. Corbett had camped at Dhikala on several occasions while out fishing or shooting with dignitaries or with friends from the forest department. The Ramganga, originating in the hills beyond Gairsain, turns southwards, flows across a narrow, thickly-forested valley near the Gairal rest house, then meanders along the northern fringe of the national park, past Jhirna, Sarapduli, High Banks and Khinanauli, before reaching the wide valley of the Patli Dun near Dhikala.

Corbett has referred quite often to the pleasures of fishing for mahseer in some of north India's submontane streams. He had fished in the Sarda, which runs along the eastern border of Kumaon that separates India from Nepal, and practically in all the rivers of Kumaon, besides the Alaknanda in Garhwal (while hunting the Rudraprayag man-eater) and as far west as the Jhelum in Jammu and Kashmir. But he reserves his most effusive praise for what appears to be the Ramganga in his story 'The Fish of my Dreams' from *Man-Eaters of Kumaon*. Corbett does not disclose the name of the river, but anyone who has trekked down the banks of the Ramganga would have little difficulty in recognizing the descriptions in his story. Besides, there are a number of clues the hunter left behind: first, that he had been fishing here in the late 1930s and 1940s; second, that it was here that he had been trying to photograph tigers (initially near Garuppu, then in the 'Farm Yard' and finally in the forests in the area); third, that the river ran for about sixty-four kilometres through a well-wooded valley (that is, from near Lohachaur to a point close to Khinanauli); fourth, that it was possible to sight chital, sambar, kakar and ghoral apart from black partridge and bush quail (primarily grassland birds) in the area; fifth, that both otters and pythons could be spotted in the river's clear waters; and last, while the valley narrowed so much in places that one could easily throw a stone from one bank and have it land on the opposite one (bringing back memories of Sarapduli and High Banks), it widened to nearly two kilometres in others, as at Dhikala. If I had to pinpoint the location of the area described in 'The Fish of My Dreams', I would place it somewhere between High Banks and Khinanauli on the Ramganga.

We lost little time in taking out the fishing permits (fishing was authorized in national parks until March 1989) and soon made our way along the banks of the river to the spot where it flows into the backwaters of the Kalagarh dam. I had a pair of fishing rods, one to be kept in reserve; but my friends from Bhimtal insisted with the novice's enthusiasm on having a go with the rod. Somewhat reluctantly, I set up a rod and reel for them with dough on the hook as bait and cautioned them about keeping their minds focussed on the job. Then I moved further up the river and set about casting my line. Under that November morning sun, with the forested hills of Pauri rising tier upon tier from the opposite bank and the waters of the river serenely blue with the reflection of the sky, everything I had read in Corbett's books since childhood came back in a rush— from the hooks made of bent pins to the greenheart rods, the home-made 'spoons' and the whining of the reel as a fish stripped off-line in its first rush to get away from the hook in its mouth. My reverie was, however, cut short by the sound of a splash and an exclamation of surprise from one of my acquaintances. He had apparently turned to light a cigarette and in that single moment of inattention a fish had pulled the rod and reel from his side! Further fishing was put off, for I was quite upset about losing the rod. Luckily for me, the forester who had accompanied us was an enterprising fellow. Stripping down to his underclothes, he waded out into the shallows to see if he could find the rod. After groping about for a few minutes, he located it with his toes. Then, taking a deep breath, he plunged under the surface of the water and pulled it out. Very cautiously, the rod was brought to shore and the line was reeled in, in case the fish was still on the hook. But that was not to be; for the heavy five-centimetre Bengal hook, normally used for carp, had broken at the shank, obviously by the pressure exerted by the mouth of the much larger mahseer which had taken the bait.

My friends departed the following day, leaving me to my own devices. Corbett National Park, seventeen years ago, was a very different place from the one it has become today. Only those seriously interested in birdwatching, wildlife photography or fishing, visited the park when I first came to know it. Grassland birds, including raptors, were present in large numbers, apart from the waders along the banks of the river, and especially, near the backwaters of the dam. The early part of the morning was spent birdwatching in and around the compound of the Dhikala tourist complex, for the grass was still quite tall and heavily laden with dew. From the woodland birds, such as tits, warblers, nuthatches and woodpeckers in the area, the bush warblers, reed warblers, babblers and crested tree swift in the fringes of the grasslands to the large egrets, stone plovers, spur-winged plovers, little ringed plovers and Kentish plovers near the water, with marsh harriers quartering the sandbanks and the Pallas' fishing eagle gliding across the waters, the park was a birdwatcher's haven.

On almost every one of the following four or five days that I spent there, I would rush through breakfast and then badger one of the members of the forest department staff to accompany me down to the river. Since the rest houses were all on the closer south bank of the river, this posed no problems, especially as several of the staff members were keen to go fishing as well. So, rod slung over shoulder, with my companions carrying the usual bottle with the line wound around it, we would walk down the shingle banks to the spot where the river curved slightly southwards, and get down to the serious business of fishing.

The fishing tackle had changed considerably since Corbett's time. Gone were the days of the four-metre-long greenheart rods mentioned in his books, or the carefully chosen ringal bamboo ones. Gone too were the special gut leads, the fine steel swivel and wire leads that Hardy Bros of Aldwick had been famous for and the spun silk lines so dear to Corbett. The *muga* silk lines were being nudged out since the late 1960s by a variety of monofilament nylon lines. Fishing rods were mostly being made either of light aluminium alloys or glass-fibre-reinforced material. The large brass or gunmetal reels had been largely replaced by the open-face, catcher-type, geared reels with a variable braking system. Even the copper or white metal two and a half centimetre or five centimetre spoons, with their great treble-hooks (also from Hardy Bros and, nearer at hand, from Verona & Co. or from Manton), had been replaced by a great variety of tobys, spinners and plugs of all sizes and hues from Mepps, Abu and others. Gone, most of all, was the easy-paced lifestyle of the forest department staff and of those who lived near the forest and the stream, along with their love of game fishing, exemplified at one time by the passion that men like Corbett and his friend, William Ibbotson, then deputy commissioner of Garhwal, reserved for the sport. These men thought nothing of putting aside their professional responsibilities for a while and spending up to ten days fishing along a favourite stream on their way to shoot a man-eater.

We usually fished at a spot about a kilometre downstream from Dhikala, where the river widened to more than a kilometre. Grassland surrounded us and enabled us to spot big game well in time, so that if the situation warranted it we could make good our escape and live to tell the tale. If we preferred a quick, short excursion, however, we made our way down to the vicinity of the pump tower, right next to the rest house, and slowly drew the spoon or toby from behind the bushes and through the shallow waters. The mahseer, most of them weighing about half a kilogram, would make a dash for the spoon and invariably get snagged on the hook. Since I did not have a car to move around in and time was short, we refrained from walking upstream towards Khinanauli. Besides, if one did proceed in that direction, the jungle encroached on the riverbanks and the possibility of coming across a tiger or elephant at any point along the five-kilometre stretch of forest road between Dhikala and Khinanauli was a very real one. Besides, an overnight halt at the Khinanauli rest house for the purpose of game fishing wasn't an option, for only forest officers on official duty and dignitaries were eligible to reserve rooms there. High Banks, the point where the river runs through a fifty-metre-wide gorge and abounds in fish, lay a further five kilometres upstream. The distance was too great to traverse on foot and the stretch provided no cover.

Down by the boulders and shingle banks flanking the river, we shared with Corbett the many delights the place had to offer despite the gulf of half a century that stood between us and the legendary hunter: the enormous blue dome of a sky flecked with curly white wisps of cloud, the Pauri hills rising in rows of green and grey against the horizon, the blue-green waters of the Ramganga gurgling past, the occasional call of the chital and, high above us, like a speckled kerchief afloat in the breeze, a solitary pied kingfisher. The forest guard or labourer who had gone out with me would unfurl a short length of the line wound around the bottle and, whirling the heavy spoon overhead, would cast it, the line spiralling off from the end of the bottle and the spoon landing with a soft 'plop' about sixteen metres away. He would let it sink for a couple of seconds, then draw in the line, hand over fist, and wind it back around the bottle in one neat motion. Some distance away, I too would be casting my line into the water. After a couple of hours we would either return from our outing empty-handed but content, or triumphantly bearing a fish weighing anything between one and three kilograms, along with several twenty-five-centimetre-long brown trout, a species of fish that seems to be fatally attracted to spoons and spinners. It was neither the catch itself nor the need for lunch or dinner that lured us to the riverbank. What had us in thrall was nature's irresistible appeal that had endured over the years, linking one man's experiences with another's dreams over a time span of five decades.

While writing about the forest streams he came across, Corbett often mentions the pythons and otters he saw. During my many visits to the national park, spread over several years, I came across pythons only twice. On both occasions, the snake was coiled up on the shingle bank, eyes shut, luxuriating in the warmth of the sun and too engrossed in life's simple pleasures to spare even half a glance for the uncouth human intruders who had come to violate its privacy. Every now and then, otters would make an appearance, scurrying over the grassy stretches of the *chaurs* or rippling through the waters of the Ramganga, scattering the shoals of fish in all directions.

Surprisingly enough, Corbett makes no mention of the mugger crocodiles we came across while fishing in the Ramganga. It could well be that in the hunter's time the reptiles were fewer in number in this area or had migrated here later, attracted by the deeper waters of the Kalagarh dam which was constructed in the 1960s. When we went fishing, however, there were so many of them that we occasionally had to abandon our chosen spot and select another, for they would always approach our particular stretch of the river, attracted perhaps by the repeated plops of the spoons in the water. We noticed quite a few, basking in the warmth of the morning sun, quite inoffensive on the face of it.

In fact, we had merely to approach within nine or ten metres of where they were lying to prompt them either to slide into the water and disappear, or float nearby, half-submerged, with their snouts and greenish-yellow eyes above the surface of the water, as though they were keeping a watch on us. Although the muggers normally left us alone, I did get a sufficiently nasty shock once when I was fishing in a pool across the river from Dhikala. On that occasion, one of these creatures had suddenly swum up so close to where I had cast my line that when it surfaced it was within a metre of me! We also caught sight of some gharial, narrow-snouted reptiles, basking in the sun. As for our apprehensions about encountering the stray tiger or elephant, they weren't entirely unfounded. Occasionally, as we made our way down to the river, we would hear loud snarls (quite possibly of mating tigers) or roars emanating either from the forests across the river or from the hills behind us. Only once, however, did a tiger come down a forest road through the grasslands bordering the river, calling as it did so. Of course, we lost little time in pulling in the line and wobbling off to the rest house on our bicycles. The twin elements of unpredictability and danger (Corbett would surely have been amused by it all!) added the spice and zing of adventure to our fishing expeditions.

Corbett had, of course, camped here on several occasions and had enjoyed fishing in the Ramganga, as I did seventy years later. Inspired by my fascination with Corbett, I tried in the next few years, as far as it was possible for a complete outsider to do so, to acquaint myself with Kumaon and the areas and landmarks he had made immortal in his accounts, starting from the places he stayed in as a child right up to those where he had hunted in his later years. I measure the success of my explorations—however limited—not in terms of the amount of information I gathered, but in the indescribable joy of discovery that I experienced.

The First Man-Eaters

In the opening chapter of *Man-Eaters of Kumaon*,
Corbett discusses at length why tigers turn into man-
eaters. He writes that although there may well have
been around 40,000 tigers in India at the turn of the
nineteenth century, only a few turned away from their
natural prey of chital, sambar and pig and took to
killing and consuming human beings for survival. The
country's population was then merely about a fourth of
what it is today. Large tracts of forest lay under the
protection of either the government or the native rulers
administering the states. Hunting regulations were
strictly enforced, with 'open' and 'closed' seasons clearly
demarcated. Moreover, poaching remained at negligible
levels. People travelling alone or in small groups through
the jungles, either on work or merely on their way to
the nearest *haat* (local bazaar), were less at risk from
wild beasts than from thugs and dacoits. In fact, 'The
Law of the Jungles' in Corbett's *My India* is an amazing
tale of two children who lost their way in the jungles,
inhabited at the time by at least five tigers, eight
leopards and a number of bears and snakes, and

returned home unscathed.

Corbett firmly believed that tigers turn to human prey only when they are incapacitated by age-related infirmities or injuries sustained in encounters with other animals or in accidents, or inflicted by human beings. Handicapped by their physical infirmities, these carnivores are unable to match the speed and reflexes of their natural prey and prefer humans who, they discover, are far easier to hunt. Another reason which leads tigers to prey on humans is the scarcity of small game in the area they frequent or the depletion in their numbers due to extensive poaching. Although the hunter bestows on the Champawat man-eater the dubious distinction of having been the first of its kind in Kumaon, Olive Smythies and J.F. Carrington Turner (a forest officer in Kumaon) have written in their respective books, *Tiger Lady* and *Man-Eaters and Memories*, that man-eaters were known to have roamed the area for a long time. An interesting observation has also been made by F.W. Champion (a forest officer in the 1920s, posted in the then United Provinces) in his book, *The Jungle in Sunlight and Shadow*, published in 1934. Champion writes that the twin phenomena of a rising tiger population (owing to these cats being regarded as 'royal' game and considered a protected species along with the one-horned rhinoceros) and the scarcity of small game like wild boar and deer (because of extensive poaching by the locals) in the terai region of Nepal adjoining Kumaon had driven these carnivores towards the Kumaon foothills in search of their natural prey. Unfortunately, the tigers native to the area did not take kindly to this encroachment on their territorial rights and forced the 'migrants' into the upper reaches of the Kumaon hills where prey was scarce or much harder to come by. How far these factors explain the repeated appearance of man-eaters in eastern and central Kumaon in Corbett's time is anybody's guess. But they seem to be as valid a reason as any. It should be borne in mind that because their urge for survival is supreme, man-eating tigers and leopards continue to hunt other game and even domestic livestock even while they prey on humans. Besides, they can easily consume between fifteen and twenty kilograms of meat in a single sitting. In fact, a hunter can and often does turn this need to his advantage by using a calf or a semi-adult buffalo as bait to lure a man-eater to a spot where he can shoot it easily. Corbett is known to have adopted the strategy on countless occasions.

Significant too is the fact that Jim hunted his man-eaters mainly in areas situated at elevations ranging between 1500 metres and 2400 metres, where the carnivore's natural prey was hard to come by. It is therefore quite possible that tigers in this area were forced to go after smaller game like kakar, pig and even porcupine. Ghoral, the alternative game, mainly confined themselves to the steep, grassy hillsides. At that elevation, oaks, chestnuts and rhododendron bushes give way to pines and deodars and the undergrowth is sparse, making it difficult for a predator the size of a tiger to stalk its prey without being detected. Encounters with porcupines often led a tiger to retreat from the scene of battle with serious injuries to its paws and legs from the porcupine's quills. The wounds would then fester, causing the carnivore great agony and undermining its ability to hunt its natural prey in the future. Thus would be born another man-eater.

Corbett made some interesting observations about the physical condition of the man-eaters he shot when he skinned their carcasses. A gunshot wound, for example, had shattered the right canine teeth of the Champawat man-eater; the Mukteswar man-eater was blind in one eye and had nearly fifty porcupine quills embedded in its right leg; the Rudraprayag leopard was old, with short, rough hair, worn-out teeth and a gunshot pellet in its chest (apart from some injuries sustained later); age had taken its toll on the Chowgarh tigress too—its teeth were either worn out or broken off and its claws either split or snapped short; the Mohan man-eater had a festering sore from numerous porcupine quills buried deep in its left leg; the plight of the Talla Des man-eater was quite similar—it had almost twenty porcupine quills embedded in its right leg; the lower right canine tooth of the Chuka tiger had probably been broken by a gunshot pellet (several pellets were found elsewhere in its body); and the Thak man-eater had, apart from other pellet wounds, a buckshot wound on its left shoulder that had become septic. Corbett has not left any record, however, of the wounds, if any, of the Panar leopard and the Kanda man-eater.

The hunter mentions in his writings that while he was serving in the railways (roughly between 1893 and 1918), he would take a month's leave every year to visit Kaladhungi and Nainital. It was but natural that

Jim should hanker for the hills, forests and wildlife he had grown up surrounded by and loved so much. Sometimes he would use these periods of leave to go after man-eaters when the district administration called upon him to do so. The first occasion on which he was asked to shoot a man-eater came about in 1907 when the local authorities commissioned him to shoot a tigress he would later refer to as the Champawat man-eater. Corbett writes in *Man-Eaters of Kumaon* that the animal had already killed more than 200 people in Nepal before it was driven out by the local residents and was reported to have killed some 234 people in Kumaon subsequently.

Champawat is a major hub of eastern Kumaon on the main highway that leads today from Tanakpur in the foothills to Pithoragarh, the gateway to the eternal snows separating Kumaon from Tibet. From Tanakpur, which is accessible by metre-gauge railway from Pilibhit just the way it used to be in Corbett's days, the road cuts through dense sal forests, travels up past Sukhidang and along a ridge to Champawat, perched at an elevation of about 1500 metres. The place once enjoyed the privilege of being the seat of power of the Chand dynasty whose kings ruled Kumaon around the mid-seventeenth century. Overrun by the Rohillas in the eighteenth century, Champawat was recovered by the British from the Gorkha invaders from Nepal in the early nineteenth century. There is a reference to the Chand rajas in Corbett's writings, and when I first visited the area in 1997 I discovered that one of the most important relics of that era was the fort located about a kilometre down the Champawat–Devidhura road. It now houses the tehsil (sub-divisional) office. Close to it stands the Nangnath–Baleswar complex of temples built by the Chand rajas. These combine the typical hill architecture of sloping eaves with sculptures that are characteristic of temples in the plains. As the crow flies, the town lies about thirty kilometres from the Kali river (also known as the Sarda as it flows through the lower stretches of this terrain) that separates India from western Nepal. In Corbett's time, Champawat was a tehsil town; it is now the headquarters of a district bearing the same name.

Whether the tigress had indeed been driven out of Nepal in quite the way Corbett has described is a moot point; tigers tend, after all, to be territorial creatures and it would have taken the persistent efforts of a very large contingent of people, covering all points where the tiger could 'break back' and reverse direction, to have flushed it out successfully and banished it from the area altogether. It is more likely that the tigress found the pickings easier on the western side of the Sarda. Why she should have moved so far west, though—easily another fifty or sixty kilometres—is again a bit of a mystery.

News of the man-eater had reached Corbett around 1903, when he was out shooting with another hunter. He had not, at the time, paid much attention to the matter, presuming that any one of the seasoned hunters who were after it, would duly account for the animal. Moreover, his railways job at Mokameh Ghat must have kept him busy. It was apparently Berthoud, then deputy commissioner of Nainital, who succeeded in persuading Corbett in 1907 to hunt the man-eater. The very fact that Berthoud should have approached Jim to undertake this responsibility, following several unsuccessful attempts by other hunters to bag it, is evidence enough that Jim's reputation as a shikari was by then fairly widespread within the administration. It also struck them, perhaps, that pursuing a man-eater called for specialized knowledge and experience that were beyond the average hunter of pig and deer and of tigers flushed out during a beat. Corbett frankly admits in 'The Champawat Man-Eater' that fear often dogged him while he was pursuing this man-eater, his first, especially when he would sit out at night waiting for the animal to turn up and imagine it lurking in each and every shadow cast by the surrounding trees. He even recalls with a touch of humour how at times his teeth chattered as much from fear as from the cold, and refers to an incident where he was startled out of his wits by a covey of kaleej pheasants rising suddenly from behind some bushes he was passing, such was the state of his nerves at the time.

There are two approaches to the area in which the Champawat man-eater was operating: one involves using the metre-gauge railway line eastwards from Haldwani via Pilibhit to Tanakpur and travelling over the foothills up towards Champawat; the alternative is to travel on foot or on horseback, directly from either Nainital or Almora and over the hills via Mornaula, Devidhura and Dhunaghat. An old road—the Sherring Road—connects Almora to eastern Kumaon. In all likelihood, it was along this road that Jim travelled when he received news of a fresh kill by the man-eater. That he did not come up from Mokameh or Gorakhpur, where he would have been working, but from Nainital, where he was perhaps on leave, is quite clear from his account and from the promptness with which he reached the site. But despite that it took him five days to cover the 120 kilometres.

This route lies, for the most part, at an elevation of around 1500 metres to 1800 metres and is lined mainly with chir pines (*Pinus roxburghii*) and a few deodars (*Cedrus deodaru*), with the occasional oak and chestnut thickets or local shrubs scattered around. Apart from the picture that emerges of the place from Corbett's writings, it is rather difficult to imagine what the terrain was like in his time. Of course, when I visited the area many years later, the presence of human habitation had significantly increased and large stretches of land had been given over to cultivation. However, the road from Champawat to Devidhura was still far from becoming a busy thoroughfare. Bullock carts were not an uncommon sight on this route, and only a couple of buses, outbound and inbound, plied it twice each day. If you missed one bus, you would have to halt overnight either at Champawat or at Devidhura. The average tourist confines himself either to the Nainital–Bhimtal–Ranikhet–Almora circuit or to the Almora–Kausani–Binsar area. The more adventurous explore the Pithoragarh–Munsiyari region. The road, though it does go through some ghat sections, is not quite as dangerous as some of the other mountain roads in Kumaon with their steep inclines, blind corners and sharp bends. Distinct from most other regions in Kumaon, the Champawat area consists of a succession of shallow, boat-shaped valleys sheltered between hills, topographical conditions that are favourable for a fair amount of settled agriculture. It may well have been the reason for the Chand rajas selecting Champawat as the seat of their administration.

Unlike the road between Tanakpur and Champawat, with its sharp gradients and hairpin bends, or the road which links Lohaghat and Pithoragarh, the road connecting Devidhura and Champawat is fairly smooth and hugs a ridge lying roughly on an east–west axis. If you look across towards the north, you can see the hillside gently falling away to a wide valley. Beyond that rises the undulating silhouette of more hills. There is not much forest en route, except for the thickets mentioned earlier. Near and around Devidhura, however, there is some tree cover. Corbett has written about orchards and tea gardens in the area. While I did come across apricot and pear orchards, though not sizeable ones, there was little evidence of tea gardens, at least along this route. What interested me more, naturally, was that the initial fifteen to twenty kilometres along this stretch from Champawat comprised the main beat of the man-eater and that during its 'reign' people were terrified of using that road. It was true, however, that the tigress had also seized its victims from areas lying east of Champawat where, incidentally, it was shot by Corbett. I found this terrain to be very different from that in the west. Cut up by short, steep valleys and ravines, the trails crossing through this area covered rougher ground. What added to the difficulty of crossing such terrain were the hills falling away to the Kali river, further east. The place was thick with deodar trees rather than pine. The vegetation, even when I visited those parts in 1997, was quite dense. Because of its topography, the population on the eastern side was sparse in comparison to the areas lying west of Champawat.

Less than four days after Corbett's arrival in Champawat, he encountered the man-eater during a beat in a shallow valley encircled by a high girdle of hills and roughly enclosed by a pair of ridges lying to the south and north. A narrow stream that trickled down from the west cut through the shallow valley for about a kilometre. Reaching a high, rocky ridge that lay right at the end of the valley in the east, it turned sharply northwards and drained out through a narrow gorge at that end. Jim's plan was to get a group of local people to shout and beat drums and generally create a racket on the hilly ridges to the south. He presumed this strategy would force the man-eater to try and make its exit through the narrow gorge, while he lay in wait for it near a grove of pine trees on the northern slope. Soon after the beat commenced about mid-day, the animal appeared in front of Jim, a little to the right and some distance from the gorge. As luck would have it, the tehsildar accompanying Corbett fired at the man-eater, causing it to break back. Corbett soon discovered that the tigress had actually circled around and appeared in front of him, slightly to the left. She leaped across the stream, apparently making for the gorge, just the way he had anticipated. A couple of bullets from Corbett's .500 modified cordite Martini Henry rifle (the one he had reportedly bought from a sailor more than fifteen years ago), fired from about twenty-five metres away, hit home, wounding the animal severely. The hunter mentions here that he was carrying exactly three cartridges: two for firing at the man-eater and the third for a contingency. This may have had something to do with his habit of economizing on cartridges and his confidence in his skill of getting his quarry with a single shot to the head. So, it was with an empty rifle that the hunter faced a mortally wounded tigress, which may still have had enough life in her to attack him. Fortunately for him, the tigress, instead of charging Corbett, turned and headed away across a nullah. The hunter followed up with a shot from the tehsildar's gun, which he had rushed back to retrieve, but the tigress was by then already on the verge of death. On skinning the tigress that night, Corbett found that its upper and lower right canines had mostly been broken off by an earlier gunshot wound. It could well have been the main reason for her having turned into a man-eater. Corbett left for Nainital the next day, completing the two-day journey (100-odd kilometres) on horseback. Going by his later hunts, his pursuit of the Champawat man-eater was short and sweet.

As is to be expected, Champawat today is quite different from the way it used to be in Corbett's time. Trade is an important concern and you have villagers

from far and near coming in to buy and sell produce
and to conduct business at the tehsil office. They have
little time to spare for visitors and certainly not for
those with seemingly absurd queries about a certain
tiger shot by some Englishman in the remote past. It
was only on the way back from a trip to Pithoragarh
that I would discover a small notice written on a
milestone just outside Champawat, informing visitors
that the place where the man-eater had been killed by
Corbett was close by. This turned out to be more hype
than truth—rather like the 'Corbett Falls' near
Kaladhungi, promoted as a tourist spot. The shopkeepers
in the area kept assuring me that the place where the
Champawat man-eater had been shot by Corbett was
close by, but no one actually took the initiative of
directing me to the spot. The town had expanded by
about a kilometre and I took the road that twisted and
turned over streams and ravines before clusters of pine
and deodar appeared. But where was the 'amphitheatre'
of hills that Corbett had referred to in his writings? In
the mass of hills and ridges to the east of Champawat,
it would have been impossible to locate the exact spot
without some marker having been put in place
immediately after the event. Some locals claimed to
know more about the matter than they actually did and
the intention, I realized, was less to deliberately mislead
the visitor than to please him. But a little probing
revealed that they had either obtained the information
second- or third-hand at best, or were unfamiliar with
the description of the terrain left by Corbett in his books.
In fact, as I was to learn later from Mrs Kiran Verma,

who along with her brother Mr P.K. Verma is the present owner of Gurney House, even the shooting of the Thak man-eater in 1938 by the legendary hunter had not caused much of a stir either in Kumaon or in Nainital. Going on shoots for big game during the dry months between November and April was a fairly mundane affair for many families living in the Kumaon hills and it is obvious that no public acknowledgement of Corbett's achievement in slaying the dreaded killer was ever made.

&

In March 1910 Corbett went out to hunt his next man-eater, the Mukteswar tigress.

Once again, Corbett had come to know of the havoc the animal was wreaking quite a while before he actually set out to shoot it. His lack of personal interest in the matter stemmed from his belief that local sportsmen would put an end to its reign of terror. After the man-eater had killed about twenty-four people and life in the small town of Mukteswar, especially in the well-known Indian Veterinary Research Institute, had been seriously disrupted, Jim was once again called upon by the local administration to shoot it. (It has never ceased to intrigue me as to why Corbett should have deviated from a simple and straightforward chronological narration of his efforts to shoot man-eaters and, instead of including the episode involving the Mukteswar man-eater in *Man-Eaters of Kumaon*, published in 1944, chose to relegate it to *The Temple*

Tiger and More Man-Eaters of Kumaon, published ten years later.)

Mukteswar, as a glance at most maps of Kumaon will show, lies slightly west of the mass of hills, lakes and forests that constitute the heart of the area. The snow-clad peaks of the Kumaon Himalaya—Trisul, Nanda Ghunti, Panchchuli and Hathi Parbat among others—rise majestically across the horizon, a mere eighty kilometres away as the crow flies. As Corbett tells us in his books, Mukteswar itself stands on a ridge that runs roughly east to west and is located at a height of about 2500 metres, offering a spectacular vista of the peaks. Although he writes that most of the ridges run roughly from east to west (or vice versa, depending on one's vantage point) as disciplined fold mountains ought to, the fact is that far from appearing neat and well-ordered the landscape here is a chaotic mess of ridges and spurs that seem to run helter-skelter in every direction. In and around Mukteswar, the vegetation is mostly chir pine and deodar, with an undergrowth of local shrubs, while at lower elevations and in places with high levels of humidity, oak, chestnut, poplar and rhododendrons naturally predominate.

It took Corbett no more than a day or so to determine that the animal that had killed a bullock near Badri Sah's apple orchard (the hunter was well-acquainted with Sah) was, indeed, his quarry. He decided to take a chance at shooting it by sitting up on a small tree overgrown with wild rose creepers that overlooked the kill lying about four metres away. By the time the tigress appeared at the kill, however, dusk was fast approaching

and a gathering mass of clouds had already blocked
out the light. Corbett decided to brave the odds and
aim his rifle (once again the .500 Martini Henry) at the
animal, relying for accuracy on the sound of the tiger
feeding at the kill. He would literally have to play it by
ear. He moved his head to one side and then to the
other, trying to locate the exact spot where the tiger
was. I have always wondered why Corbett attempted
such a risky shot, which might have been wide of the
mark and sent the animal fleeing to an area far away;
except that he had infinite faith in his faculties and
always tried to stretch the limits of his skill with the
rifle. Corbett later discovered that he had actually
missed the tigress by just about fifteen centimetres. The
animal gave him some anxious moments for the rest of
the evening, growling and prowling around in the
vicinity if he so much as moved on his perch on the
small tree. At around 11 p.m., a thunderstorm broke
and the tigress moved away to seek shelter from the
rain.

The following day, Corbett arranged a beat by groups
of local people in the area where a pair of narrow
ravines, running steeply down the face of a nearby hill,
joined up close to a stream. Although it seemed for a
while that for some reason or the other the beat had
been aborted, the tigress suddenly appeared across a
field that was lying fallow about twenty-five metres
away just when Corbett and the beaters had decided to
take a break and enjoy a smoke. As soon as the animal
passed behind some trees and shrubs, Corbett pursued
it, hoping to catch up with it without being detected.

He came close enough to the tigress to hear it feeding at an old kill a few metres away. Along with the beater who had followed him, the hunter sat huddled together for sometime until they spotted the tigress moving up the hill on the opposite bank of a ravine. Jim chanced a hurried shot, at which the tigress whipped around and came at him in what then appeared to be a determined charge. He was able to aim a second shot at its neck and shoulder when the animal was less than a couple of metres away. The heavy bullet caused it to veer off to one side, past the hunter, and it was already dead when it tumbled into a small stream that ran below. As he was to find out later, the animal had been badly wounded in an encounter with a porcupine. It had lost an eye and a number of hard quills were embedded in the muscle of its right foreleg. There was every reason to believe that these injuries had turned the animal into a man-eater.

My sole visit to Mukteswar was a rather brief one. A single bus leaves Haldwani for Mukteswar in the morning, reaching the place just in time for lunch. It returns to Haldwani the same afternoon. In the short interval between my arrival in Mukteswar and the time of departure for the return journey, I was unable to locate Badri Sah's apple orchard. Besides, the town has developed to such an extent, with the jungles around it being cleared as a matter of course, that it is hard to imagine Mukteswar as an area once terrorized by a man-eater. In fact, the couple of resorts that have come up in the area dispel any aura of the original Corbett country that might linger. The saving grace is a lovely, if distant, view of the Himalaya and the Indian Veterinary Research Institute, which Corbett mentioned in his books and which still maintains a large, green, if unkempt, campus. However, for the people passing through its gates, the thought that a man-eater had lived around these parts more than eighty years ago, and continues to live on in a famous hunter's equally famous book, is far from their minds.

Ꮟ

In 1910, around the time he shot the Mukteswar man-eater, Corbett was deeply immersed in his railway assignment. He was also looking after the hardware and real estate business of F.G. Mathew & Co. in Nainital, although he was assisted in this venture by his mother and sisters. Later that same year, he would go out and hunt the Panar man-eater, initially in April, and then again in September. The hunter's quarry this time was a man-eating leopard that had created havoc in areas bordering the Panar river, east of Almora, then headquarters of the Kumaon region. It is worth noting that for the third time in succession, Corbett would be aware of the activities of a certain man-eater long before he actually accepted the responsibility of shooting it (on this occasion in as far back as 1907, when he was out hunting the Champawat man-eater). Coincidentally, as was the case with the story about the Mukteswar man-eater, Corbett would include his account of the Panar man-eater in *The Temple Tiger*, published forty-four years after he shot the leopard in 1910.

Kumaon's two major rivers are the Kosi and the Panar. The former flows down from the north, past Bageswar and Almora, before turning west, while the Panar courses down at some distance east of Almora before turning further eastwards towards Lohaghat. At Ghat, it meets up with the Saraju coming down past Pithoragarh. Since the man-eater was operating in the valley of the Panar, Corbett named it after the river for easy identification.

The Panar valley was relatively isolated during Corbett's time. I was pleasantly surprised, when I visited the area more than eight decades later, to find that it had remained much the same. The road between Almora and Pithoragarh, which skirts the north or left bank of the river, is hardly frequented, except for the few buses that ply during the day. The road runs over a series of ridges and spurs resulting in many sharp turns. At times, the slope leading down to the river is so steep that a downward glance can be quite frightening. Far below, perhaps more than 300 metres, the river looks like a thin silver ribbon threading its way past a succession of spurs. Towards the east, near Ghat, patches of sal forest still survive, while pollarded sal, poplar and oak are visible in the upper reaches. As you approach Almora, however, chir pines and deodar predominate and in places the forest cover is fairly thick. Along the steep-flanked valley lies a cluster of huts or small villages, often separated from each other by a distance of four or five kilometres. Even when I visited the valley so many years after Corbett, there were mere foot trails running up the hillside to connect the scattered settlements, and the villages that lay along the motorable road were few and far between. It was to this area that Corbett had come in April 1910, along the Almora–Devidhura road which follows the south bank of the river.

It didn't take the hunter much time to locate the tracks of the man-eater. Following the trail, Jim came to a place where he was confronted by a tragedy. A young woman had been seized by the man-eater from her room in a dwelling about forty kilometres from Almora. The man-eater had caught her by the throat, but she managed to utter a cry that alerted her husband in the nick of time and enabled him to pull her away from the predator by summoning great courage and nearly superhuman effort. The wounded woman had lain unconscious in the room for the rest of the night, while the leopard repeatedly growled and scratched at the bolted door. Never one to let go of a chance to bag a man-eater, Corbett decided to sit up for the animal in a small recess on the ground floor of the hut. Although a jackal called once in alarm from about a kilometre away and the hunter watched the shadows carefully throughout the night, there was no further cause for alarm.

Corbett was back in the area in September the same year. This time he had chosen the route via Panwanaula along the Almora–Pithoragarh road. For a few days, he searched for the leopard among the scattered villages on the north bank of the Panar. Then, on hearing about a kill on the opposite side of the river, Jim and his helpers undertook the arduous trek over hill and spur, down one valley and up another, before they could cross the river, that too, with considerable difficulty, to go over to the south bank. For the next couple of days, the hunter tied a pair of goats as bait for the leopard. On the third day, following a brief bout of malaria, Corbett sat up on a stunted oak tree that had grown at an angle over a terraced field and stood at a short distance from one of the baits. Instinct apparently warned Jim that his perch on the oak tree was unsafe and led him to direct his men to cut some hard, thorny shoots and tie them tightly around the base of the trunk. Around sunset, Corbett heard the calls of a scimitar babbler and a white-throated laughing thrush some distance away; these birds did, at times, sound an alarm when predators were in the vicinity. Shortly afterwards, the goat started bleating. A few minutes later, the hunter felt a tug on one of the thorny shoots: the man-eater had arrived and sensing that someone was up on the tree, was trying to get at him! Unable to pull away the shoots, the leopard tried another tactic: it caught them in its teeth and started tugging at them violently, growling loudly all the while. Only a seasoned shikari like Corbett, with a deep knowledge of predators and immense faith in his firearm, could have survived such an encounter. Besides, he had a twelve-bore shotgun loaded, in all likelihood, with LG ('large game') cartridges, ideal for a close shot at a soft-skinned predator like the leopard.

After a few minutes of this deadly tug-of-war, the leopard jumped down to the terrace and ran towards the bait; it obviously wanted its dinner one way or the other! The bait, a white goat, was some twenty-five metres away. Jim could just about make out a dark blur against the pale skin of the goat as the carnivore seized its prey. In those days, there were no electric torches to shoot by. So Jim aimed as best he could and fired his shot at the shadow. There was a grunt from the leopard and it seemed that it had fallen straight down into the field below. After about a quarter of an hour, when all was silent and the leopard was presumed to be dead, men started emerging from the nearby huts, carrying torches fashioned out of pinewood splints. Making their way to the tree on which Corbett was sitting, they cut away the ropes with which the shoots had been fastened to the tree. Then they helped him down and led him, in the flickering light cast by their torches, to the spot where the bait had been tied. As the group arrived at the edge of the field and attempted to look over at the spot where the leopard had apparently fallen, the animal jumped up and snarled menacingly at them. Corbett's companions dropped their torches and bolted. Fortunately, Corbett was a consummate marksman. Using the uncertain light of the flickering torches now lying scattered on the ground, he managed to pump a bullet at close range right into the animal's chest, thus ending the leopard's career as a man-eater.

Along the Almora road, on my way from Lohaghat to Jageswar, the magic name of Panwanaula appeared around a bend in the road, not far from the place itself. The Panar runs far below, deep in the shadows of the valley. Unlike other areas in Kumaon which are frequented by tourists, this region still has a fair amount of forest cover comprising mainly pine and deodar. Corbett hasn't left too many clues about the actual village where he had shot the Panar man-eater. Looking down into the gorge, however, and gazing at the trails that seem like fine pencil marks etched here and there between far-flung huts and clusters of oak and dwarf rhododendron along the slopes, it isn't too difficult to visualize how desolate this place must have been in the hunter's time. Even the Jageswar temple complex, though frequented by pilgrims during the day, falls eerily silent as evening descends on the forest. It doesn't take too great a stretch of the imagination to be overcome by the feeling that here, within the folds of the hills, lurk quite a few leopards. The shooting of the Panar man-eater was rather special in the sense that although Corbett had been stalked by some of the man-eaters he had hunted, such as the Chowgarh tigress and the Mohan man-eater, the Panar leopard was perhaps the hunter's first experience of a man-eater deliberately going after him in such a determined manner. That the carnivore's intentions were eventually thwarted was entirely due to Corbett's sound instincts and the diligence of his helpers in tying the thorny branches firmly to the oak tree.

Hunting his first man-eaters had been relatively easy for Corbett and, with the exception perhaps of the Panar leopard, almost like the game shoots he used to go on. By a strange quirk of fate, the man-eaters that Jim was called upon to hunt in the later years, when his stamina and faculties must have been on the wane with advancing age, involved prolonged and nerve-racking stalks, especially when he himself was stalked by the man-eater. That he acquitted himself superbly despite the odds and survived to tell the tales through his books is a tribute to the man's vast knowledge and uncanny intuition about the forest and its denizens, his supreme confidence in his marksmanship, his iron resolve, and the exceptional courage that made him stand apart from the shikaris of his generation.

The Intervening Years

Having shot three man-eaters between 1907 and 1910, Jim was not called upon by the authorities to render this service again until 1926. In the first place, he was not a professional hunter. Besides, he was bound by his trans-shipment contract with the railways till about 1918. In addition to the hardware business of F.G. Mathew & Co. which kept him busy along with his real estate brokering work in Nainital, Jim also served for quite a few years on the municipal board in Nainital and introduced a number of innovations to control traffic and deforestation of the areas around the town. In 1915, he had bought the landholding rights of Chhota Haldwani, a village near Kaladhungi and devoted a good deal of his time to supervising its affairs. A couple of years after World War I came to an end, Corbett had also taken up the ownership and management of a tea garden near Berinag, north-east of Almora. Then, in 1922, Jim and Sir Percy Wyndham jointly acquired a coffee plantation in East Africa and supervised its operations.

By this time, Jim had become a man of some means and social standing. He had acquired a wide circle of friends and well-wishers, many of whom were members of the civil administration in Kumaon as well as in the United Provinces. Yet, when he turned fifty in 1925, Corbett did not opt for a life of ease and comfort. His upbringing as a child of the Victorian era, the straitened financial circumstances of the Corbett family which had compelled him to seek employment when he was only eighteen years old and his sense of responsibility towards his ageing mother and his sisters may have been instrumental in his decision to adopt an austere lifestyle. Usually dressed in khaki shorts, a half-sleeved shirt, a brown or grey serge or tweed jacket, sola topee, knee-length socks and sturdy walking shoes—the standard attire in his time of most of the forest officers with whom he was friendly—Jim often camped out in the open, fished in the streams of Kumaon and roamed the jungles that he loved, sometimes with a rifle under his arm, but increasingly, with a movie camera to capture wildlife in its natural habitat.

It should come as no surprise then that at the age of fifty, when other men would have been looking forward to a more sedentary life, Corbett chose to undertake one of the most arduous hunts he had ever been commissioned for: the hunt for the man-eating leopard of Rudraprayag. By this time, apart from the three man-eaters, he had shot several tigers and quite a few leopards. Off and on, he had heard reports of the havoc wreaked by the Rudraprayag leopard, but had not thought to follow up on them. As Corbett puts it in his book, *The Man-Eating Leopard of Rudraprayag* (first published in 1947), it was when he came to learn that Sir Michael Keene, chief secretary of the United Provinces at the time, was trying to persuade some hunters to go after the man-eater that he decided to take up the task himself

Interestingly, Rudraprayag lay way to the north-west, up in the hills of Garhwal, quite far from Corbett's usual beat in the forests of Kaladhungi, Garuppu, Kotabag, Nayagaon and the maidans of Rudrapur. It is difficult to improve on Corbett's description of the route from Hardwar via Lachhman Jhula (the famous suspension bridge over the Ganga near Hardwar) to Rudraprayag that the pilgrims used in the early years of the twentieth century for their journey on foot to the temples of Badrinath and Kedarnath. The entreaties of hordes of beggars still resound in the ears of visitors to Hardwar and the macaque monkeys which rule the area near Lachhman Jhula are just as insistent and mischievous as they used to be in Corbett's time. The devotees of Baba Kalakambli, who wore the black blanket typical of the hills and thus gave the order its distinctive name (the hunter refers to them as the '*kalakambli-wallahs*'), still tend to those in need and in distress in some of the towns and villages in Garhwal. Corbett writes that the walk up from Rishikesh (for some inexplicable reason he alludes to it in his book as 'Rikikesh') to the town of Srinagar would take about three days, a distance of almost 100 kilometres covered nowadays in four hours flat by the buses roaring up the ghat sections on this route. Yet, in spite of the obvious rise in population, the increasingly larger tracts of land given over to cultivation and the growth of quite a few villages into townships, Garhwal, with its matchless vistas of the majestic snow-clad Himalaya stretching from the Yamunotri peaks in the west to Panchchuli in the east, remains largely unchanged even seventy years later.

In his book on the leopard he had set out to hunt, Corbett offers a graphic picture of the sheer terror that had reigned in the villages around Rudraprayag between 1918 and 1926 because of the depredations of the man-eater. A severe epidemic of influenza had reportedly swept over the region in 1918. In the absence of appropriate medical treatment and suitable medicines, people had perished in large numbers and could not be properly cremated because of the shortage of firewood and manpower. The village folk apparently disposed of the dead by simply placing burning embers in the mouths of the deceased and pushing them off a cliff some distance from their village. Leopards are not above scavenging if deprived of their regular prey and, as Corbett speculates in his book, it was possible that the man-eater had consumed some half-burnt corpses and acquired a taste for human flesh. Be that as it may, between 1918 and 1926 (when it was shot by the hunter) the man-eater had chalked up a total of 125 victims. The pitiful tales of the shepherd boy plucked by the man-eater from the midst of his herd of goats inside the cattle shed, the man snatched by the predator from his home while enjoying a smoke with his friend, the sick woman dragged out from her room by the leopard through a narrow window and the young Gujjar girl killed right inside an enclosure while surrounded by buffaloes, come alive in Corbett's book with an immediacy not every writer is capable of achieving. The power of the hunter's narrative involves the reader in the feeling of panic that held sway over the affected villages in the area so many years ago and effectively conveys the seriousness of the threat posed to their inhabitants by the man-eater.

This was the situation that Corbett walked into when he arrived in Rudraprayag in 1925, at the end of a ten-day trek from Nainital via Karnaprayag. He may well have taken the Nainital–Ranikhet–Bhatrojkhan–Gairsain–Karnaprayag route, covering a distance of about 300 kilometres, undoubtedly an arduous journey. It involved a long detour from Nainital to Ranikhet, followed by the next leg of the trip across the Kosi to Bhatrojkhan along steep spurs and ridges and on to the valley of the Ramganga near Ganai before crossing over the hills to Gairsain and moving further along the Pindar to Karnaprayag. Of course, it is just possible that Corbett may have taken a more northerly route via Almora, Garur, Gwaldham and Karnaprayag, but the distance he would have had to cover would have been about the same. The word *prayag* means 'a confluence of rivers'. The Alaknanda and Mandakini rivers, fed by the snows of the Himalaya lying farther to the north, converge at Rudraprayag before flowing southwards to meet up with the Bhagirathi at Deoprayag. Corbett describes with characteristic flair the roughness of the terrain, especially to the east of

Rudraprayag on the way to Karnaprayag, with its spurs, ridges and strips of terraced cultivation along the hill slopes. For nearly ten weeks, Corbett scoured the countryside, part terraced cultivation, part grasslands and jungle including dense scrub forests, in a quest for the man-eater, visiting village after village during the day and sitting up at night either on one of the pillars of the suspension bridge spanning the Alaknanda (on one occasion he was forced to do this for twenty days at a stretch) or over a human kill or cattle bait. Corbett has described in some detail his many attempts to kill the man-eater by poisoning portions of a kill, setting a large gin trap and even by tying up his rifle near a kill in the hope that the leopard would push against a trip-cord, triggering the release of the bullet that would kill it. He writes also of the futile attempts by local holy men to rid the area of the predator through prayer and 'magic' spells. In fact, Corbett had even been followed by the man-eater while on his rounds to inspect the kills. On one occasion, both he and Ibbotson were in grave danger as they left a kill and were forced to trek quite a distance in the dark, because the lantern they were carrying had been extinguished when it impacted with a rock. Weeks of this kind of strain had taken its toll on Jim and, tired in body and spirit, he had made his way home a few weeks before Christmas.

By the spring of 1926, however, he was back. This time, he took the train to Kotdwar (possibly along the Lalkua–Bareilly–Moradabad–Najibabad route) and continued on foot via Pauri to Rudraprayag, thus managing to save a good deal of time and energy.

Once again, he tried all the options, from tying up baits, sitting up over kills and poisoning them to setting a mechanical trap, but to no avail. Once, when Corbett was sitting up on the branches of a pine tree, waiting for the man-eater, he even tried to induce the animal to come within shooting distance by imitating the call of a leopard, but had to suffer the mortification of hearing it make its way towards the tree and then veering off at the last moment while it was still some distance away. There were times when the hunter himself was in danger of being attacked by the man-eater, as on the occasion when he was keeping vigil over a kill and it started to rain. Corbett had to cover nearly half a kilometre in the dark, walking over rock-strewn terrain before he could reach the road, fearing every moment that it might be his last if the man-eater were to come after him. While recounting the incident, the hunter describes it as a 'night of terror' and confesses that he had seldom been as afraid for his life as he was on that occasion.

Ultimately, it was the predictable behaviour of the man-eater that led to its undoing. Corbett had observed that once every five days or so, the leopard used the road between Rudraprayag and Golabrai, a hamlet situated about three kilometres down the pilgrim route on the east bank of the Alaknanda. The hunter decided to sit up for the animal on a mango tree that stood a short distance from the pilgrim shelter in Golabrai and tied a goat as bait on the kuccha road that ran right past the tree. Having done so for ten days at a stretch, Corbett realized that he was almost at the end of his tether. On the eleventh night—2 May 1926 to be precise—the leopard apparently arrived at the spot shortly after 9 p.m. It began to stalk the goat that had been tied up about six metres from the foot of the mango tree. As the leopard rushed at the bait, the tinkling of a small bell tied around the goat's neck warned Corbett about the predator's proximity. Forever alert, he instantly switched on the torch attached to his rifle. The beam of light fell on the leopard as it lay sprawled on its belly, facing the goat. Jim pulled the trigger. Under the impression that the wounded animal had leapt over the goat and tumbled down the slope that fell away from the edge of the road, he remained on the tree for the rest of the night, trying, somehow, to keep himself comfortable. At the crack of dawn, he climbed down and noticed a streak of blood on a rock nearby. It reassured him that the man-eater had been mortally wounded and he found the leopard dead and cold in a hollow in the ground about forty-five metres down the hillside.

There was much rejoicing that morning among the villagers; even Ibbotson was hardly able to contain his feelings of relief. Later in the day, thousands of local people came to see for themselves that the 'evil spirit', as they had believed the man-eater to be, had indeed been vanquished and as a token of their gratitude to their saviour they showered Corbett's feet with the flowers they had brought with them.

It was more than seventy years after this event that I was able to visit Rudraprayag to make an attempt to locate the spot where the hunter had bagged this most feared of man-eaters. From the insignificant hamlet it used to be in 1926, Rudraprayag has now grown into a small town, with electricity round the clock, several small hotels, a couple of resorts and even an intermediate college thrown in for good measure. One of the main reasons for its development is perhaps its location at the intersection of the road running in a north-easterly direction via Karnaprayag towards the famous shrine of Badrinath and the one moving roughly northwards via Gaurikund towards Kedarnath. The jade green waters of the Alaknanda rush in from the east, past Karnaprayag, shortly after it is joined by the Pindar which comes down from the snows farther east. The dark emerald waters of the Mandakini course down from the north and a suspension bridge still straddles the river at Rudraprayag. The suspension bridge over the Alaknanda has been replaced by a large steel cantilever bridge connecting the Kedarnath road with the one coming up from Hardwar via Srinagar and Deoprayag. The other suspension bridge that Corbett writes about, located in his day at Chhatwapipal, about nineteen kilometres up the Alaknanda towards Karnaprayag, is no longer there, obviously having failed to survive the onslaught of time. Of course, there are several suspension bridges along the way to Karnaprayag and Corbett may well have been referring to any one of them. It was on either side of the Alaknanda, between Rudraprayag and Chhatwapipal, further east, that the man-eater of Rudraprayag had held sway.

During my visit to the area, I found the terrain along

the left or south bank of the Alaknanda to be tough going, with its high, sharp ridges, deep gorges and ravines in between, exactly as Corbett has described it. This region is overrun by scrub jungle (also mentioned by him in his writings), possibly because of its thin subsoil, thickly seamed with bare rock in many places and its scanty rainfall compared to that in the areas lying further east. In fact, the vegetation included the euphorbia cacti and the Phoenix palm, commonly found in more arid regions. Large pine groves, usually seen at higher elevations in Kumaon, are absent here. A few stragglers line the ridges, while the ravines down below, closer to the river, hold small patches of mixed jungle. These are, in fact, the typical features of leopard country, which does not favour heavy jungle.

Although Rudraprayag has evolved into a much larger place, people there tend not to loiter outdoors after dark, though this could be due as much to the chilly weather as to any other reason. Except for the occasional 'whoosh' of a car passing along the road, evening noises in this place are confined to the tinkling of bells in the temple that stands at the confluence of the Alaknanda and the Mandakini. I stood for a while on the bank of the river as night descended around me. The velvet-thick darkness and the soft murmur of the river aroused in me an eerie feeling of something waiting to happen. The hills seemed to have fallen into a stupor, undisturbed even by the call of a nocturnal bird.

Morning, and the bright sunshine it brought with it, improved my mood significantly and after breakfast I took off down the road that skirts the left shoulder of the Alaknanda towards Chhatwapipal (yes, this has also withstood the ravages of the years) for about five kilometres before reaching a point where the river narrows. Here the water foams and fumes around the many large boulders sitting solidly on the riverbed before rushing on. Could this have been the spot, I wondered, where Corbett had fished for mahseer while taking a much needed break from the stress of stalking the man-eater of Rudraprayag for days on end? It seemed eminently possible; gorges and boulders are rarely known to change position, even over several decades. Farther up the river, I saw a couple of men at the water's edge, fishing rods in hand. For a moment I thought whimsically that perhaps the grandfather of one of those men had been the young boy who had helped Corbett land his catch on a particular day nearly eighty years ago.

The following morning I decided to visit Golabrai, which stands on the left bank of the Alaknanda, about five kilometres down the road that connects Rudraprayag with Deoprayag. I boarded a bus at the local bus stand that is today a tangle of jeeps, Maruti vans, Sumos, mini buses, fruit vendors and shops selling utensils and other provisions. Surrounded by the chaos it was hard for me to imagine that in 1926 this very road used to be the nocturnal haunt of a man-eating leopard. The bus I was travelling in overshot my stop and I got the opportunity to stroll back from the point where I had got off. At the very spot where the pilgrim shelter used to be located in Corbett's day (evident from a photograph in the first edition of *The Man-*

Eating Leopard of Rudraprayag) now stands the office of the local panchayat samiti. No one seems to have a clue as to the whereabouts of the pundit who would offer shelter to the pilgrims travelling on that route. However, the old mango tree still survives, an ancient witness to the padded footfalls of the man-eater, the strangled cry of a victim snatched from the vicinity of the pilgrim shelter and the swift intake of breath as the hunter sitting on one of its branches, his nerves taut with anticipation, pulled the trigger. Behind me rose the hill with its ravines and spurs, down which the man-eater had made its way on that fateful night of 2 May 1926.

As I stood before the mango tree, the sequence of events that had led to the death of the animal played itself out in my imagination, as if I had actually been an eye-witness to it all. The road to Deoprayag, now metalled, with cars and buses roaring up and down at frequent intervals, runs at a higher elevation than the mango tree, not below, nearer the river, the way it used to in Corbett's time. Some enterprising official has had a small plaque erected about ten metres down an almost 150-metre-long slope descending to the Alaknanda below. The message painted on it is as follows: *On this very spot was killed the man-eating leopard of Rudraprayag by Jim Corbett on 2 May 1926*. Thus preserved for posterity is the only accurately identified spot where a man-eater was shot by Jim Corbett. Although the man-eater was killed in 1926 and the book based on the incident was written in 1947, it is quite possible that between 1965 and 1970, when the plaque was apparently put up, there were still people around who knew about the shooting of the leopard, either directly or from others, and could identify its precise location. It must have helped, of course, that the area faithfully conforms in appearance to Corbett's description of it. As I left Rudraprayag for Hardwar the next morning, I raised a hand in salute as the bus passed the mango tree in Golabrai as a tribute to the great shikari.

&

In the early 1930s Corbett was called upon by the authorities to shoot three more man-eaters: the Chowgarh man-eater (shot by the hunter in 1930) in central Kumaon, the second in the foothills of Pauri and the third in western Kumaon. A few believe that he shot the second of these man-eaters in 1932 at Kanda and the third in 1933 near Mohan. It is my opinion, however, that the Mohan man-eater was accounted for in May 1932, while the Kanda man-eater was shot in May 1933. This is borne out by the fact that as Corbett's account of his shooting of the Mohan man-eater comes to a close in his book, the hunter himself tells us how he proposes to describe the way in which he bagged the third tiger, the Kanda man-eater. Moreover, my contention seems to be supported by the petition dated 18 February 1933 that some villagers in the Pauri–Garhwal region (within which Kanda lies) presented to Corbett, pleading with him to deal with the man-eater that had been terrorizing them since December 1932.

The Kosi, springing from the foot of the snow-clad Trisul in the central Himalaya, flows south, past Almora, before sweeping westwards. Emerging from western Kumaon below Ranikhet, the river is forced, once more, to turn its course south, as it runs up against the hills and ridges of Pauri. Fed by the snows from the mountains of eastern Chamoli, the Ramganga, on the other hand, flows roughly southwards. Then, emerging on the opposite side of the high ridges above Gairsain and unable to find a way out, the river turns south and east through the shallow valley of Ganai (also known as Chowkhutia) before entering the Patli Dun valley at the foot of the Pauri hills, from which point it flows west. The point at which the Kosi turns south and the Ramganga veers to the west is separated by hardly ten to fifteen kilometres as the crow flies. During my bus journey to Gairsain en route to Rudraprayag, I noticed that the ghat sections on the hills above Mohan, which lies on the Ramnagar–Ranikhet road, were densely clothed in sal and mixed forests along the lower reaches. As the bus climbed up, they gave way to vast stretches covered by oak and chestnut groves. However, once we had passed the road that led down to Baitalghat, the vegetation thinned to pine forests and grass, with a few thickets of shrub sprouting near and along the steep rocky ridges and deep gorges that characterize the topography of this region.

Mohan and Kanda are situated around forty to forty-five kilometres north-west of Corbett's winter home in Kaladhungi. Corbett begins his tale of the Mohan man-eater with a compelling description of how an elderly woman, who was cutting grass along the slope with her companions, lost her footing and fell on to a ledge a little way down the hillside when the tiger suddenly charged at them. The account of the young girl who kept the injured woman company as they anxiously waited for a rescue party from the village to come to their aid and how she was seized by the tiger from the ledge right before the old woman's terrified gaze shortly before the rescue party arrived is nothing short of tragic.

Corbett was commissioned by the district administration to shoot the tiger a few years after it had acquired a taste for human flesh. He arrived in the area in May 1932, at the height of summer. After the hunter had spent about five days tracking the tiger by tying a couple of buffaloes as bait at different points, the man-eater seized one of the animals and dragged it several hundred metres down and across a hill, to a point a few metres from a large rock that stood on the hillside. Corbett discovered the kill some distance from the rock and began stalking the tiger. He reached a grassy patch from which he realized the tiger had just moved off, apparently in search of shelter from the heat of the sun. He surmised that the animal had, in all likelihood, moved to the shade of a fallen tree that lay further down the hillside. Approaching it very cautiously, Corbett found the tiger asleep on a narrow ledge that lay along the far side of the tree. The hunter had agonized over the dilemma of whether it would be ethical to shoot a sleeping animal, but managed to appease his conscience by persuading himself that he was, after all, out to kill a man-eater that had taken several human lives. However, Jim could not help describing the sight of the sleeping tiger's belly as it ceased to heave rhythmically once the two bullets from his rifle bore through its forehead and blood trickled out of the fatal wounds.

It was more than fifty years after Corbett had shot his man-eaters that I visited Mohan. Travelling by bus from Haldwani to Ramnagar, one passes Kaladhungi right at the foot of the Nainital hills. From this point onwards, the road moves away from the hills and meanders through the terai, north of Garuppu and Bajpur (mentioned several times by Corbett in his writings) before turning north. It soon approaches the hills of Sitabani before crossing the Kosi over the barrage at Ramnagar. The road from Ramnagar to Mohan runs along the west bank of the Kosi, almost parallel to a high cliff on the river's opposite bank. Several tourist resorts have sprung up in the last ten years or so along the Kosi, where in Corbett's time there had been only the occasional village or just a couple of huts, set amid cultivated fields between patches of forest that descended to the edge of the water. As mentioned earlier, the temple to Garjia Devi rises from a huge rock squatting right in the middle of the river. Even in the mid-1980s, it was possible to catch sight of a solitary tusker or even an entire herd of elephants crossing the river from the Sitabani forest to the safety of the Corbett National Park whose boundary the road skirts for some distance. Mohan lies at the foot of a high ridge running roughly in a north–south direction along the west bank of the Kosi and about seven kilometres beyond the Dhangari gate of the national park on the road linking Ramnagar to Kumeria and Bhatrojkhan. Large stretches of sal and mixed forest characterize the vegetation in this area. Although Corbett called the tiger he shot here 'the Mohan man-eater', after the village of the same name, his description of the terrain in which he killed it matches the topography of the area that lies about six to eight kilometres further north. Kathkanaula (referred to as 'Kartkanaula' by Corbett) lies to the north-east of Chimtakhal, which in turn is a short distance north of the Durgadevi forest check post that stands on the road from Ramnagar via Mohan to Morchula and beyond.

As I trekked up the ghat section from Mohan to Durgadevi through the sal forests, I felt a shiver run through me and I realized that it wasn't entirely due to the crispness of the early morning air. There was far less traffic on this road than on the main Mohan–Ranikhet route, and on the two trips I made down that lonely road, first to obtain an overall impression of the area and then to find the way to Kathkanaula, I met people only once on each occasion. On the first, I came across a couple of herders, accompanied by their pack horses, a pair of guard dogs and the long-haired hill goats peculiar to the region. The picture they presented perfectly matched the descriptions Corbett offers of the region in his writings. On the second occasion, I passed four local women hurrying home with baskets full of the grass they had collected from the hillside. Since the road lay to the west of the north–south ridge above Mohan, sunlight penetrated the area rather late in the day, hovering for a mere hour or so before it moved away again. A small stream kept me company as the road climbed past dark ravines so overgrown with dense forest that I couldn't resist the impulse to look over my shoulder repeatedly and to speed up my pace when I had to walk past the dark patches of forest bordering the stream.

The forest staff (consisting of just two men) assigned to the Durgadevi check post were obviously surprised to see me, a stranger to these parts, walking up the deserted road. The tea they offered seemed to me far more than a mere expression of hospitality. Apart from refreshing me, it served as a kind of reassurance that I was not the only human soul in that part of the world. The trek to Chimtakhal involved a climb up a sharper gradient and was quite exhausting. The place lies on a kind of plateau. A small village has sprouted here with a couple of government offices lending it a semblance of civilization. It was over another cup of tea at a stall here that I learnt that Kathkanaula was still six kilometres away, across another ridge to the east. This part of the route was less hemmed in by forests and was flanked by stretches of terraced cultivation, but the effort required to cover the distance on foot was quite beyond me that morning, for I had to take a train from Ramnagar in the afternoon.

The problems I encountered while trekking through the area seemed inconsequential when I recalled the obstacles Corbett must have had to overcome while out hunting the Kanda man-eater. Kanda is situated approximately west of Mohan, on a steep ridge that lies further west and runs roughly in an east–west direction along the right or north bank of the Ramganga. Today, it falls within the boundaries of the Corbett National Park and overlooks the Patli Dun valley, the location of the Dhikala tourist complex. This is one of the few areas that have, by and large, remained unchanged since Corbett roamed through them. A perch on the stone parapet bordering the tourist rest house in Dhikala is the ideal place for enjoying the entire vista of valley spread out below, with the Ramganga weaving its way through the grassy banks and the ridge of Kanda visible across the river, a towering greyish-green mass in the distance. Herds of chital and hog deer can often be seen moving gracefully around the river's sandbank between the sissoo saplings and the grass patches. With a little bit of luck, you just might catch a glimpse of a herd of wild elephants or even a tiger crossing one of the streams some distance away on the opposite bank of the river.

Corbett does not offer any information on the route he chose while pursuing the Kanda man-eater. In all probability, he proceeded through Ramnagar, passed the Durgadevi check post on his way to Mohan, then crossed the Ramganga to make his way past Domunda and Lohachaur to the Kanda rest house high up on the ridge. Even today, this area is heavily forested and infested with elephants and other wild animals. Corbett arrived here in May 1933 and spent about a fortnight looking for the man-eater in the neighbouring jungles. Then news reached him of a buffalo kill made by the tiger and he quickly decided to take the opportunity to track down the animal and shoot it. He followed up the kill to a narrow valley on the north face of the ridge with a boulder-strewn stream running through it. As he approached the kill, Corbett had a premonition that the tiger was close by. His hunch was correct, for the man-eater had, in fact, been a mere six metres away, concealed in the dense undergrowth. It moved away, however, running at full tilt up the hillside before Jim could aim his rifle at it. It paused, however, to spring up a rock face about fifty metres away and Jim seized the chance of getting in a quick shot and assumed he had wounded it badly. But this was obviously not the case, for the tiger, after falling back, seemed to recover and galloped off around the shoulder of the hill. Jim was back at the buffalo kill the next morning and was happy to see that the tiger had apparently returned to it during the night and eaten some portions of it. While pondering where and when to sit over the kill for the man-eater, he heard the tiger's call. Although Corbett tried to trick it into approaching the spot by imitating the call of a tiger, the man-eater refused to cross beyond a certain point, wary perhaps of the area in which it had been shot at.

Corbett decided to sit over the kill by climbing up a tree that grew at an angle from a steep bank flanking the stream. As night descended on the area, the tiger, which had apparently been in the vicinity and had watched the hunter climb the tree, came out to investigate. Corbett was alerted to the presence of the predator by the alarm call of a langur, and as he positioned his rifle to train it on the tiger which had approached the tree from a different angle, the animal growled deep in its throat. After a short while, however, the tiger moved away, coming around again to feed on the kill. Corbett managed to spend the night on one of the branches of the tree. Just as dawn was breaking and his men called out from higher up in the valley, the tiger, which had it seemed been resting near the kill, ran off across the face of the hill to Corbett's left. Jim attempted a shot in spite of the weak light and the bullet struck home. The tiger spun around and, with a deafening roar, came for the tree on which Corbett was perched. This gave him the opportunity to give it another shot, and this time the bullet struck the animal straight in its chest. The tiger hit the tree trunk and fell into one of the pools formed by the stream that flowed at a slightly lower level. It struggled out of the water and somehow managed to move some distance down the ravine before collapsing, lifeless, into another pool.

Although the ridge at Kanda was easily visible from Dhikala, I could not make my way there because the four-wheel-drive vehicle that would have enabled me to do so was unavailable. Nevertheless, one morning, I took a hired jeep across the Ramganga to the southern foot of Kanda. Riding over a wooden causeway and then over the *chaur* turned out to be quite an experience. Soon, we came to a deep valley running from north-west to south-east down the shoulder of the Kanda ridge. Being familiar with the description of the area given by Corbett in his writings, it struck me that this could well have been the backdrop against which that sad tale had played out, so many years ago, of an anxious father risking his life by going out at night in search of his missing son, unaware that the latter had been taken by the man-eater. This tussle between man and nature could not have occurred at a more likely spot. While out exploring the area on elephant-back one afternoon during a subsequent visit in 1988, we came across a large male tiger that asserted its territorial rights in a highly aggressive manner by refusing to give our elephant right of way and snarling quite impressively to make its point. I was happy I had chosen an elephant that was stout-hearted enough to resist bolting at the first sign of trouble!

Even today, the Kanda area, with its high, hogback ridge, ravines and thick forest, is the habitat of a fair number of tigers. It is seldom visited, except by forest officers. In fact, in the 1970s and 1980s, Corbett National Park witnessed human kills and incidents of mauling by tigers although its population of chital and sambar, the natural prey of the big cats, is significantly large. That a man-eater had roamed Kanda half a century ago, wreaking havoc as it went and bringing untold misery to the rural folk of the region should therefore come as no surprise. As in other regions of Kumaon, however, destiny seems to have compensated for the absence in those days of an adequate support system to take care of contingencies arising from attacks by man-eating predators. With neither a sufficient number of forest personnel available for surveillance nor medical facilities at hand, not even transport to ferry the victim of a savage attack to hospital in time for emergency treatment, the villagers of Kanda would have had no one to turn to, had it not been for a godsend: Jim Corbett, armed with his weapon, his wits and his iron will.

The Later Man-Eaters

Corbett's exhausting and seemingly interminable treks through forbidding terrain, the days and nights he spent out in the jungle exposed to the elements and the danger of attack by wild animals, sometimes without any form of sustenance other than wild berries, and the perennial tension he was under from having to be on his guard at all times while pursuing a man-eater, add up to a prodigious feat of endurance that seems altogether incredible. When Jim undertook his most difficult hunting assignments, he was over fifty-five years old, a time in one's life when the coordination between eye and hand usually begins to slacken, the legs and back tend to buckle under the strain of long-distance treks over hill, dale and jungle, and the prospect of lounging in an armchair, swapping reminiscences of past hunting experiences with like-minded friends, seems infinitely more appealing than a cramped position on the branch of a tree waiting for a bloodthirsty man-eater to make its appearance.

But then Corbett was no ordinary shikari. By the time he was fifty-five, the hunter seems not only to have had more time to devote to his pursuit of man-eaters, but to have been more driven to ridding Kumaon of this menace. Between 1907, when he shot his first man-eater near Champawat, and 1926, when he bagged the man-eating leopard of Rudraprayag, Corbett had accounted for just two other man-eaters: the Panar leopard and the Mukteswar man-eater. Between 1929 when he was fifty-four, and 1938, when he had crossed sixty-three, he had shot half a dozen more man-eaters. Some of these hunts happened to be among the toughest Jim had undertaken, in terms of the length of time he was outdoors, the distances he had to cover, the effort involved in negotiating hilly terrain as he trekked through the day without a break and the sheer mental strain of being on the alert day after day while stalking a dangerous carnivore, that too one which had acquired a taste for human flesh.

I can well appreciate the kind of endurance test these hunts must have been for the hunter. For there had been a time, when camera in hand I had explored forest trails and game tracks in many of India's national parks and wildlife sanctuaries for that elusive 'perfect' shot of a wild animal in its natural habitat. The sheer thrill of tracking animals, including big game such as tigers, leopards and bison, was intoxicating indeed, though I must confess that I usually gave elephants a wide berth. But the experience brought home to me the kind of demands that being out in the wild alone made on a man. I came to realize that only an individual with high levels of physical fitness and a rare degree of motivation could succeed in tracking wild animals for six or seven hours a day and that too for four or five days at a stretch. The nerves tend to fray after that and the entire exercise degenerates from a fulfilling activity into a tiresome chore.

Corbett, of course, enjoyed several advantages over others. Firstly, his intimate knowledge of the jungle and the ways of the animals came in handy as did the regularity of his excursions, whether motivated by pleasure or by necessity, which kept him on his toes and enabled him to perfect his 'junglecraft'. Secondly, he had toughened his constitution from the time he was a child by following a regimen of long treks along the hilly roads of Nainital and in the foothills. Added to this were his mental fortitude, his commitment to providing much-needed respite to the villagers of Kumaon from the depredations of man-eating predators, and perhaps the urge to take up the challenge of testing his wits and skills against those of a seasoned opponent on the latter's own ground. These factors, put together, constituted an unbeatable combination.

Predictably enough, after Corbett's death, doubts had been expressed by certain forest department officials involved in Project Tiger over the truth of the claims he had made in his writings. Had the hunter really shot that many man-eaters, they asked. There were even those who questioned the possibility of there having been any man-eaters at all in Kumaon during the years Jim spent there. As mentioned in the opening chapter of this book, these arguments are not only countered by the conviction with which the accounts of Corbett's experiences in the jungle are written, but also by the evidence presented by his hunting companions (ranging from gun-bearers and tehsildars to deputy commissioners) and by those who had joined him after a shoot. Interestingly enough, I discovered several references to Corbett's pursuit of man-eaters, with special emphasis on the man-eating leopard of Rudraprayag in F.W. Champion's book, *With a Camera in Tigerland* (1927). The author also uses quotes from the *Pioneer*, a widely-read newspaper in those days, referring to Corbett's success in bagging man-eaters. References to Jim's hunts have also surfaced in official documents and in the local and overseas press. In his book, *Man-Eaters and Memories*, on forest life in Kumaon in the 1920s and 1930s, J.F. Carrington Turner has explicitly described Kumaon as 'the land of man-eaters' when referring to the man-eater at Gwaldham (which he shot) and those at Mukteswar and Kala Agar. When Lord Wavell was viceroy of India, he had sought out Corbett's earlier writings and stories about the hunts, lending credence to their authenticity. Moreover, the hunter had on occasion gifted people, including some of his publishers, the skins of some of the man-eaters he had shot. To infer, therefore, that in Corbett's time, there may have been as many man-eaters in Kumaon as there were in Bastar in the 1950s (according to R.C.V.P. Noronha's book *Animals and Other Animals*, published in 1992) would be perfectly in order. In ridding large areas of Kumaon of the menace of man-eating carnivores, Jim also established the benchmarks, as it were, for physical fitness, mental fortitude and raw courage that, as far as I know, have yet to be surpassed by other hunters, at least in this country.

As Corbett aficionados are well aware, he had shot the Chowgarh tigers and the man-eaters of Mohan, Kanda, Chuka and Thak between 1930 and 1938. By this time, he had matured into a hunter with greater confidence in his skills and intuition, far removed from the more tentative young man he used to be during his pursuit of the Champawat, Mukteswar and Panar man-eaters in 1907 and 1910, when he was beset by doubts about his capabilities of being able to account for the predators. It is also significant that whereas during the earlier hunts Corbett had relied on either organizing a beat and flushing the man-eater out from its cover or enticing it to approach a bait so that he could shoot it over the kill, in the later years he preferred to stalk his man-eaters, in a way perhaps pitting his own instincts against the predators'. In his books, Corbett writes of his commitment, publicly acknowledged during a conference with district officials in February 1929, to shoot the three tigers that were causing great distress to the people of Kumaon. Of these carnivores, one was the Chowgarh tiger which had killed more than sixty-four people in central Kumaon between 1925 and 1930 in villages as distant from each other as Padampuri, Khanshio (Corbett's version is 'Khansiun'), Okhalkhanda (referred to as 'Ukhaldunga' in the hunter's writings), Kala Agar and Dalkania—all lying to the east and south of the tourist resort in Bhimtal. The two other tigers were the Mohan and Kanda man-eaters which held sway over the western fringe of Kumaon, bordering Garhwal.

To begin with the episode involving the Chowgarh tigers, it was sometime in April 1929 (apparently, shortly after he shot the Talla Des man-eater) that Corbett took leave to hunt this man-eater. He trekked from Nainital, choosing in all probability a forest trail leading eastwards via Bhimtal and Naukuchiatal and covered nearly seventy-five kilometres in four days to reach the Kala Agar ridge, where the man-eater seemed to be concentrating its activities. The hunter has described in his books the region's dense forests of oak and rhododendron, interspersed with patches of cultivation. Almost immediately on arrival, he had set out for Dalkania ('Dalkanya' is how the locals spell it), which lies about twenty-two kilometres further east. For the next few days, Jim relentlessly pursued the man-eater which had recently killed a village cow. He spent three nights out in the open, sheltering up on a tree to keep out of the man-eater's reach. By this time Corbett had been out in the open in quest of the tigers for nearly sixty-four hours. On the third day, Jim managed to stalk the kill to a distance of about twenty-seven metres and shot one of the pair of tigers feeding off it. As luck would have it, he ended up shooting, by mistake, the nearly full-grown cub that was accompanying the man-eating tigress.

For the next ten days, Corbett scoured the country around Dalkania and the area lying to its south, proceeding towards a ridge that was the watershed for the Nandhour, which flows south past Chorgalia, located in the foothills. There had, in the meantime, been two further attempts by the tigress to snatch a human prey. Both were women. In the first incident, the woman's companions had managed to drive off the predator; in

The ruins of Arundel, Corbett's ancestral home

A view of Talla Des, on the way to Tamuli village

The gorge of the river Sarda near the Purnagiri temple,
frequently mentioned in Corbett's writings

The site where Corbett killed the man-eating leopard of
Rudraprayag

A view of the lake at Nainital; Ayarpata is situated
close to the centre, on the right

Gurney House—Jim's residence at Ayarpata

the second, both the tigress and its victim had tumbled down the hillside. Having been out pursuing the man-eater for nearly a month, Corbett decided to return home, travelling south-west this time from Dalkania via Haira Khan (about thirty kilometres away) and Ranibag (lying on the main Haldwani–Nainital road) down a forest road, which is no longer used. On the way down, Jim was overcome by the feeling that the man-eater was stalking him and actually spotted its tracks just ahead of him beside a forest pool. When his helpers arrived, Corbett brought up the rear, covering them with his rifle. A short distance ahead, the group came across a villager herding buffaloes. After asking him for directions, Corbett urged the man to hurry home, explaining that the man-eater was in the vicinity. The hunter adds that when he returned to the area a few months later, he heard from the villagers that shortly after they had left the cowherd, the unfortunate man had been seized by the man-eater. The buffaloes he had been tending had, however, driven off the carnivore and the man somehow managed to reach the village and recount his horrifying story. Although he was taken to the Haldwani hospital by his fellow villagers, he had succumbed to his injuries.

Jim came back to Dalkania in February 1930. He shot a leopard that had taken to killing cattle in the area and pursued a tiger that had attacked a bullock in a ravine lying some distance away at a lower elevation than Dalkania. Corbett sat up over the remains of the bullock and when the villagers joined him in the morning, they were surprised to find a couple of tigers lying within a short distance of each other, both shot dead by the hunter. Apparently, they were a mother and cub pair and one had followed the other to the kill. These episodes were mere diversions for Jim. Of the man-eater there was no trace, even though Jim remained in the Dalkania area for two weeks. With no leads to pursue, Corbett decided to turn homewards again.

However, at the end of March the same year, Ham Vivian, the then district commissioner, who had been touring the Kala Agar area, got in touch with Corbett and asked him to shoot the man-eater which had apparently attacked a woman cutting grass along with a few others in the compound of the Kala Agar forest rest house. Jim hurried down from Nainital, managing on the way to shoot a couple of leopards that had killed one of the buffaloes tied out as bait for the man-eater. There was, as usual, no trace of the animal he was seeking so desperately. For the next two weeks or so, the hunter explored the jungle trails looking for clues that would lead him to the man-eater he was looking for, but although he knew he was being stalked by his quarry, luck was obviously not on his side. Corbett's first and only direct encounter with the Chowgarh man-eater took place on the afternoon of 11 April 1930. Approximately to the south of the Kala Agar rest house was a forest trail that went off in a south-westerly direction. That afternoon, the hunter, accompanied by his helper, Madho Singh, and one other person, set off down the trail to tie out a couple of buffaloes as bait. Having decided to tie one of the baits near the spot where a villager's son had been killed,

Jim made his way there down a track across the valley before climbing up the opposite side. He tied the buffalo to the stump of a tree next to a thicket of oak near which the man-eater had killed the boy. He then made Madho Singh climb a tree and pretend to cut its branches, asking him to talk loudly as he went about his task, much as villagers usually did. Meanwhile, Jim waited next to a rock, not far away.

The hunter soon sensed that the man-eater, attracted by the chopping sound of the axe and the babble of human voices, was somewhere close by. The buffalo was also betraying signs of uneasiness. Corbett guessed that the tigress had approached quite close to the spot, and was standing not far below the rock next to which he himself was waiting. Shortly afterwards, the sound of a twig cracking a short distance away, as though a heavy animal had stepped on it, indicated that the tigress had for some reason veered off and descended from the slope. Jim decided to work up to the opposite side of the hillside from where he could keep his eye on the buffalo bait, in case the tigress came back for it. So the group went nearly back 100 metres down the trail they had used earlier to a point where it ran across a ravine. Opposite the trail was a large patch covered by a heavy tangle of bushes and undergrowth. Corbett had no intentions of negotiating the stretch of thick vegetation which afforded the tigress both cover and the opportunity to ambush the party. He decided, therefore, to climb down into the ravine, move along its open, sandy banks for some distance before climbing up again at a spot where he was clear of the dense undergrowth. As Jim was about to enter the ravine, a nightjar (a nocturnal bird that usually nests on the ground) rose with a flutter of alarm from its nest that lay on a rock to one side of the ravine. The hunter discovered that the nest contained a pair of eggs. As an avid collector of birds' eggs, he could not resist picking them up. Holding them in his left palm, he cushioned them with bits of moss to prevent them from breaking. Then, with the nightjar's eggs held carefully in his left hand, Jim walked down the ravine's sandy bed and came to a cascade that plunged down for nearly four metres. During the rains, the water rushed down the ravine with great force, smoothing out the surface of the rocks over which it flowed. Handing the rifle to one of his companions, Corbett slid down the smooth rocks to the bed of the ravine.

Hardly had he landed on the sand, when his two helpers also jumped down beside him, shoved the rifle into his hands and asked him excitedly if he had not heard the tigress growl. He had not. This could have been due to the sound being muffled by the scraping of his clothes against the rock and the thud with which he had landed on the sand. The three men were now standing on the bed of the ravine which, at that spot, was shaped like a narrow rectangle about fifteen metres long and three metres wide. Behind them rose the smooth, rocky slope. To their right, a large, flat rock leaned slightly towards them. A fallen pine tree sprawled across the end of the ravine. As Jim stepped cautiously across the sand, the nightjar's eggs still cradled in his left hand and the rifle held in the crook of his right arm and across his chest, and turned the corner past the slab of rock, he came face to face with the tigress. It was crouched there, half-hidden behind the rock, gathering itself for a spring. Corbett's description of the scene in *Man-Eaters of Kumaon* captures every heart-stopping second of his final showdown with the Chowgarh tigress. According to the hunter's account of the incident, his gaze never wavered from the animal, which was looking at him from a distance of a little over two metres, as he turned the barrel of his rifle almost in slow motion, repositioning it with his one free arm until it was pointing at the animal. Then, as if using a revolver, he loosed off a shot. Time seemed to stand still until Jim noticed a spurt of blood from the bullet-hole in the tiger's chest and the animal sank to the ground. Corbett describes those moments as a living nightmare, following which a nervous reaction set in and he felt his legs about to buckle under him. Handing the rifle to Madho Singh who was a few paces behind him, Jim managed to stumble across to the fallen pine tree and sit down for a well-earned smoke. Thus ended the hunt for the Chowgarh man-eater.

When I visited Chowgarh in 1999, I discovered that there were two different routes I could take to reach the territory the man-eater had once claimed for itself. The area lies beyond the high ridge and the thick forests of the foothills that are immediately visible to the east and north of Haldwani. The first route, which I once attempted to take, leads east from Haldwani, along the foothills of Nainital and Bhimtal to Chorgalia. According to the locals, the forest road from Chorgalia

ran, at one time, up the foothills to Haira Khan, close
to where Corbett shot the Chowgarh tiger. The forest
road I travelled up passes the Chorgalia forest rest
house along the right bank of the Nandhour before
gradually turning north and west, past the shrine of
Shanmun Thapla. Then it moves over low hills and
peters out. I found that the roads had not been repaired
for quite a few years and that the forest had encroached
on that portion of land and claimed it back for itself.
Dense mixed forests still surrounded the area and
included stretches of sal trees. The highlight of my trip
to Chorgalia turned out to be the presence of a tigress
doing the rounds of the locality with its cubs in tow,
picking up the odd bullock or buffalo left to graze in
the jungle. I passed one such kill which was stinking to
high heaven, for the prey had reportedly been seized a
week earlier. To explore these parts and not give way
to the constant urge to look over one's shoulder, as I
did, would have been an unnatural response. For the
sceptics who might be inclined to scoff at such a reaction
on my part, I would like to add that the same afternoon,
when my two local guides and I were returning from a
visit to the shrine, a tiger called several times from the
hillock behind us.

A couple of years later I tried the alternative route.
If you gaze up from Haldwani towards the north-east,
past the approximate location of Bhimtal, a series of
high, jagged ridges covered by dense forest and running
further east is visible. This approach leads along the
Haldwani–Devidhura road, up over the ghat section to
Bhimtal. The road then circles the lake at Bhimtal before

touching the villages of Vinayak, Chafi, Padampuri and Dhari, on its way to Dhanachuli. En route to Bhimtal, I noticed the sal forests and teak plantations and an abundance of haldu, toon, terminalia and other trees that generally grow in mixed forests. Chir pines appeared sporadically amid the shrub jungle and terraced fields and the occasional oak thicket or stretch of orchard. A few buses plied during the day from Haldwani, making their way past Bhimtal and Dhanachuli to Devidhura and further on to Champawat and Lohaghat. At Dhanachuli, the road split into three separate routes, one curving to the left on its way to Ramgarh and Bhowali, the second moving ahead to Devidhura and the third turning sharply to the right towards Khanshio and Kala Agar. On my way I found that Padampuri, where more than seventy years ago the Chowgarh man-eater is reported to have claimed a victim, had developed into a fairly prosperous village whose residents now earned a respectable income from growing vegetables in greenhouses!

After taking a hairpin bend at Vinayak, the road I was travelling along ran up to Dhanachuli which afforded a splendid view of the eternal snows of Nanda Devi and Trisul. After a refreshing cup of tea at a stall, I somehow managed to squeeze myself into the 'share' jeep in which passengers were already packed tight like sardines. They included householders carrying sacks of rice and vegetables, government staff going back to their assigned stations, women suffering from car sickness and children with snot dribbling from their nostrils. The road turned right (or south) along the road to Okhalkhanda. Deep ravines, steep hillsides and dark gorges appeared, first on one side of the road, then on the other. Dense thickets of oak, chestnut and rhododendron lined the road and, if you went by local reports, there was still a good number of bear, tiger and leopard, apart from wild boar and deer, in that area. After a distance of nearly twelve kilometres had been covered, the forest thinned out a little. Once we had passed Okhalkhanda and were approaching Khanshio, the road—now metalled—ran down a wide valley. The river Gola cut through this valley before surfacing once again at a much lower elevation at Ranibag, on the way to Nainital. There was quite a bit of terraced and settled cultivation in the area and Khanshio was now a village consisting of thirty-odd houses including several shops and a couple of tea stalls. To the south, towering over the village, was the Kala Agar ridge, overgrown with oak, pine and other trees. For all practical purposes, the metalled road ended here and a fair-weather road climbed the right shoulder of the Kala Agar ridge and ran further east for another twenty-two kilometres to Dalkania. The Ladhya, which flows east of the Kali, originates from one of the springs in the ridges that lie beyond the wide valley, north of Khanshio. I learnt from the local people at Khanshio that over the last fifty years or so, there had been a sharp spurt in the region's population. The forests had been encroached upon and terraced cultivation was under way in many places. There were no reports of wildlife being present in that area and it was quite possible that poaching had, to some extent, driven the game away. Corbett writes that the man-eater had taken one victim from Khanshio, but that had happened many decades ago and had long faded from public memory. Still, I experienced something of a vicarious thrill just standing in the village where Corbett had come in search of the Chowgarh man-eater.

From Khanshio, a glance up the slopes of Kala Agar—where the Chowgarh man-eater had reportedly seized eight victims—revealed deep ravines, blanketed in a cover of oak and chestnut, along with other mixed forests and trailing lianas, clearly indicating what much of the area must have been like in Corbett's time. Walking a kilometre and a half up the steeply rising gradient of the road towards Kala Agar, I noticed that the trees grew closer and closer to the road as I progressed. As the sights and sounds of Khanshio fell away behind me and I passed the dank shade cast by the crowding trees, I felt distinctly uncomfortable. Visible in the distance were a few people with a couple of pack ponies trudging slowly up the slope of the Kala Agar ridge. I knew I could follow them to reach Kala Agar, six kilometres away, but time was against me. Whether I would have been able to locate the ravine where Corbett had finally confronted the Chowgarh tiger, is something I will never know. However, the knowledge that I had come close enough, at least geographically, to the specific area was consolation enough for me.

&

Eastern Kumaon, that is Champawat and the areas to its east, holds great fascination for the nature lover.

The hills rise rather abruptly from the grasslands of the terai—now mostly under the plough—near Tanakpur. The mighty Kali constitutes the boundary between India and Nepal. The river winds its way around steep hills before rushing through deep gorges from its source among the glaciers above Askot and Taklakot, while the hills near Pithoragarh and Lohaghat offer a lovely view of the shimmering snows of Nandakot and Panchchuli, stretching to the foot of Mount Kailash, 'the churning staff of the gods', as legend has it. The lower reaches of the hills are clad in long stretches of sal forests and mixed forests consisting of rohini, ficus, terminalia and bauhinia (including the *Bauhinia vahlii*) trees that provide a haven for a variety of animals and many species of bird such as jungle fowl, pin-tailed green pigeon and white-cheeked and white-crested laughing thrushes. Oak and chestnut predominate at intermediate heights where kaleej pheasant, nuthatches, grey tits and others of the same species twitter all day. Further up, beyond an elevation of 2100 metres, chir pines and deodars proliferate. A fierce tangle of hills, ridges, spurs and ravines extends from the main road running up north from Tanakpur to the Kali in the east.

Following Corbett's order, the hunt for the Talla Des man-eater would sequentially come last, on the heels of the episodes involving the Chuka and the Thak man-eaters, all three having taken place near the right bank of the Kali, close to where the Ladhya meets up with it, about thirty kilometres above Thuligad. The Chuka tiger had boldly attacked human beings and, on one occasion, when disturbed at a kill, had slain a couple of young boys and two heads of the cattle they had been out tending. Corbett's friend, Ibbotson, who had taken charge as deputy commissioner for Nainital, Almora and Garhwal districts in 1937 and his wife, Jean, accompanied the hunter to that area in April 1937. Travelling largely on foot via Haldwani, Tanakpur and Thuligad, they followed the steep, but shorter, trail through the Sarda gorge, fishing as they went, to Kaladhunga (not to be confused with Kaladhungi), a village by the same river.

After spending about five days in the area trying to locate the man-eater, Corbett sat over a kill and experienced the mortification of watching the tiger approach the tree from afar before moving away completely. The following day he was informed that one of the buffaloes tied up as bait in a narrow ravine had been killed by the tiger. Corbett approached the ravine in a roundabout way to avoid alerting the man-eater and was able to get as close as eighteen metres to the kill. The tiger sensed the intrusion and started growling. Corbett backed off, pausing beside a ravine. When one of his companions strained for a better look at the spot, the tiger, which had been watching them from across the ravine, started up the hill. Jim chanced a shot as the animal emerged from behind some bushes. But the bullet apparently clipped through the fur on its neck, hit a rocky surface and ricocheted back, causing the tiger to fall over among some vines and shrubs. The hunter had missed a good chance of bagging the man-eater, although the shot had admittedly been a difficult one.

A couple of days later, some distance from Thak, the tiger attacked another buffalo which had been tied up as bait and dragged the kill for more than three kilometres through thick undergrowth and down steep hillsides into a hollow. Close by stood a wild fig or ficus tree which, as is common with the species, had taken root as a parasite on a larger tree, strangling it to death. About three metres from ground level, the original tree had rotted and fallen away, providing a reasonable seat for the hunter amid the fig's branches. After a frugal lunch (and the inevitable cigarette), Corbett climbed on to his chosen seat. Shortly afterwards, he was alerted to the predator's presence in the vicinity by the alarm call of a macaque and, peering around the trunk of the tree, he saw the tiger standing about thirty-six metres away, looking towards it. Obviously, it had heard the men moving around near its kill and was undecided whether it would be safe to approach it.

Over the next half hour or so, the tiger moved towards the tree cautiously and, as Jim kept absolutely still, came right up to it and lay down at its foot. Craning his head to look at the animal, the hunter was able to make out the tiger's head to his left, but the animal's position was too awkward to risk a shot. Leaning over to the left, he could see the tiger's tail and about a third of its body. Deciding, as he had with the Mohan man-eater, that sentiment had to be sacrificed when dealing with a man-eater, Corbett pointed the rifle—this time the heavy but highly effective .450/400—at the animal, looking 'under the barrel rather than over it', and let off a shot. The tiger rolled over and started to slide down the hillside, and Corbett aimed another shot at it which hit the animal in the chest. Corbett has written, with a touch of regret, it would appear, that instead of snarling or roaring with pain at the first shot, the tiger took both bullets and died without uttering a sound.

ॐ

Halfway through 1938, however, the Chuka–Thak region in eastern Kumaon would have to confront yet again problems arising from the presence of a man-eater. Forestry operations were under way, and unless the tiger was shot quickly, the felling of trees and their preparation for transport were likely to be badly affected during the dry season that would follow shortly as the woodcutters hired for the job had every reason to refuse exposing their lives to such risk. On receiving a report, therefore, in September 1938, that a girl had been killed by a tiger at Kot Kindri village (close to where he had shot the Chuka man-eater), Corbett duly set off in search of his quarry. Accompanied once again by Ibbotson, he decided to go up the gorge of the Nandhour that flows past Chorgalia. According to his account of the experience, Jim met up with Ibbotson at Chorgalia on 13 October and spent a few days fishing in the Nandhour before reaching Durga Pipal, about thirty kilometres upstream. Within a day, they were close to Chalthi, which lies between Sukhidang and Champawat, on the Tanakpur–Pithoragarh road. Ten days after leaving Chorgalia, the team reached the village of Sem, close to the confluence of the Ladhya and the Sarda.

During the days that followed, the men received reports of two kills: one of a bullock, the other of a buffalo that had been tied up as bait. The terrain with narrow and deep ravines, steep hillsides, boulder-strewn streams and sheer cliffs made a close approach extremely difficult. At one stage, Corbett approached the tigress close enough to hear her growl, but experience had taught the animal the value of caution and it made off without giving the hunting party a chance at a shot. Jim spent another three or four days on the lookout for the man-eater, but in vain. So, on 7 November, he set off for the return journey to Tanakpur, navigating once more the unforgiving terrain he had crossed to reach Sem. He covered the thirty-two kilometres or so in less than a day, that too, at the age of sixty-three, and boarded the train to Haldwani. Within a few days of his return, however, Jim received news of a fresh human kill at Thak. He hurried back to Chuka on 24 November. The next morning, he set out to tie a buffalo as bait near Thak. On the way back to Chuka, he skirted around the village of Thak and found that the tigress had stalked him all the way up to the village, passing a water trough where he had taken a drink on the way up and following him back down the valley. Only his experience of the jungle and his heightened awareness of possible danger in such terrain had seen him through that stalk.

For the next few days, the hunter tied up a number of buffaloes as bait and sat over the kills. On one of those nights, when it was approaching full moon and the jungle was flooded with light so that everything around him was clearly visible, he spotted a sambar doe with its fawn in a field close by. Corbett had been sitting in this position for about a couple of hours, when a kakar started giving its alarm call from somewhere above the village. Hardly had it stopped than Jim heard a loud, long-drawn-out cry of sheer agony from the direction of the village. It sounded like the scream of a man in excruciating pain. For a few moments, Jim was in half a mind to get down from his perch on the tree and go in search of the person who had uttered the cry so that he could help him. That he had not imagined the sound was clear from the reaction of the sambar doe which fled from the field the moment it had heard the cry. Later, when Corbett questioned the headman of Thak village about the cry he had heard the previous night, he was told that the person who had been snatched by the man-eater a few days earlier had called out in distress in much the same way. Corbett could make little sense of this strange experience and has put it down in his account as an other-worldly phenomenon defying explanation.

The hunter sat up one more night over a buffalo kill, but to no avail. The period he had set aside for accounting for the man-eater had drawn to a close and it was time for him to return to Nainital. On returning to camp, he met a throng of people who begged him to try his luck once more and tie up a couple of goats this time, for surely the tigress would prefer the tastier goat over the buffalo. The path leading to Thak went up a steep ridge. As Corbett approached the ridge, he heard the tigress call from an area some distance to his left, which lay behind a dense thicket and was intersected by narrow ravines and strewn with boulders. After a couple of hours of waiting, Corbett had had enough of the chill in the air and came down to call up his men who had taken shelter on a plot of cultivated land nearby.

Depressed and weary, the hunter started on his way down to Chuka along the path that sloped down a ridge. Shortly afterwards, he heard the tigress call, once again, from beyond a valley that descended to the Ladhya on his left. There was just about half an hour of light left before evening closed in. Drawing on his profound knowledge of the wild, Corbett decided to lure the tigress out of hiding by mimicking the call of a tiger, for he knew that the month of November coincided with the mating season for these carnivores. The tigress immediately answered his first call from across the valley. Subsequently, Jim and the animal exchanged several calls in quick succession, as it hurried in the direction of what it presumed to be a prospective mate. In his book, Corbett gives an enthralling account of the incident. He prepared to meet the man-eater near a big rock that lay at the edge of the flat piece of ground, approximately forty metres wide and eighty metres long, through which the trail from Thak cut across before sharply zigzagging down towards Chuka. He and his four helpers quickly climbed down to a narrow ledge that ran just below the rock so that he could face the path down which the man-eater was likely to arrive. While his men huddled at a spot just below where he was sitting, Corbett was somehow able to hold himself in that awkward position by sitting sidewise on a rocky ledge and keeping a precarious grip on it with his left hand. It was already becoming dark and the light would last for no more than a couple of minutes. At that moment, the tigress called again, this time from a spot in front of the hunter, a little towards the right, just behind a pile of rocks at the edge of the clearing. Corbett realized how close the animal was because he could hear the sharp intake of its breath. Then it took a couple of steps to its right and called once more. All Corbett needed to do was pull the trigger the moment the tigress's head appeared over the rocks. The first shot hit the animal on its right cheek, the second, in its throat. Its lifeless body came to rest very close to the rock behind which the hunter and his men had been sheltering. Thus ended a heroic and memorable hunt, which not only rid a large part of eastern Kumaon of the menace of a man-eating predator, but also marked the end of Corbett's hunts for man-eaters. He was, by then, sixty-three years old and had been hunting man-eaters for close to thirty-two years.

When I wanted to visit the area in 2000, inquiries at Tanakpur drew a blank and it was only at Sukhidang, about twenty-two kilometres up the road to Champawat, that I got a lead from the owner of a small wayside stall, about two kilometres from Sukhidang, on the ridge overlooking the village. He belonged to a branch of the family of priests assigned to the task of tending the Purnagiri shrine and was originally from Chuka which lay another thirty kilometres to the north-east. The man sized me up sceptically before making the candid pronouncement that the trek I was contemplating would be quite beyond me, for the trail went so steeply up before descending that a city-bred person with little experience of negotiating hill tracks would take at least two days, if not three, to cover the distance. He went on to claim that the locals covered the distance in about six or seven hours and that the local postmen took turns to deliver the mail from Sukhidang to Chuka before exchanging the mailbag on the return journey with another postman coming up from Chuka at a point midway. He added that there was still quite a bit of wildlife in that area by way of sambar, chital and wild pig (which made cultivation—or whatever little there was of it—even more difficult). But there had been no reports of tiger sightings in recent years. He then redirected me to Chalthi, which stands on the Ladhya, a further twelve kilometres from Sukhidang en route to Champawat.

Another bus ride and, a couple of hours later, I was at Chalthi. Inquiries near the steel cantilever bridge spanning the Ladhya (also known as the Chalthi in this area) revealed that a forest road, now rarely used, ran along the south or right bank of the Ladhya to Chuka. Before I had covered a kilometre down this track, I was convinced that my stamina would not measure up to even a quarter of what Corbett's had been at the age of sixty-three. The number of boulders I would have to circumvent to complete the journey and the trees and shrubs I would have to force my way through were more than the one-man army I represented could take. It would require porters and guides to surmount all the obstacles on the way and make it in one piece to Chuka, still twenty-eight kilometres away. I was sorely disappointed, but could not help marvelling, once more, at Corbett's enormous physical stamina and mental resilience that had taken him into the hostile terrain frequented by the man-eater. I would learn later, that in April 2003, Dr A.J.T. Johnsingh of the Wildlife Institute of India, Dehra Dun, had taken a group down the forest road along the Ladhya, managing to reach Chuka and Kaladhunga, where the old bungalow (in which Corbett and Ibbotson had put up) still stands though it is now in a rather dilapidated condition.

ॐ

The Talla Des man-eater had been hunted down earlier, in 1929 (Corbett, it seems, may have been a little confused about the dates). This particular hunt had especially strained Corbett's physical and mental resources and had taxed to the extreme his knowledge and experience of the jungle. To aggravate matters, the hunter had suffered a major injury to his left ear in February 1929, when he was out on a shoot with guests in the Bindukhera area of the terai and a high-velocity rifle had been accidentally discharged right near his head. Jim had suffered excruciating pain and although he received medical treatment, it was clear that his eardrum had been damaged. To top it all, serious infection had set in within the ear causing painful internal inflammation that had nearly closed his left eye.

Unlike the average hunter, Corbett had decided to carry on regardless, pursuing the Talla Des man-eater in April 1929 to prevent himself from brooding on the persistent pain caused by his injury and also, he writes, to spare his family from having to witness his agony. He was alone except for his trusted assistant, Madho Singh, and some Garhwali coolies, as he travelled via Kathgodam, Bareilly and Pilibhit to Tanakpur, and from there onwards, through the Sarda gorge at the foot of the Purnagiri hill, to Chuka. The area where the man-eater was operating lay beyond a high ridge to the north of the Ladhya from where the hunter was directed to another village, Talla Kot. Here, the man-eater had killed a woman a few days earlier. While he was exploring the area with the dead woman's son, someone called out to Jim from the village situated at a higher elevation. The man informed him that from his vantage position, a red object was visible in a terraced field further below. This could be anything, from a dry patch of fern to a deer or even a tiger. Creeping along one of the terraced fields, the hunter and his companions arrived at its edge and looked down. About 110 metres below them, in a grassy patch across a shallow ravine, a pair of tigers lay side by side.

What followed next was a remarkable display of marksmanship. Setting his sights and cushioning the rifle—his trusty .275 Rigby—Corbett first targeted the tiger lying further away from him. Once the bullet had hit home, the animal remained immobile. The second tiger was, however, up in a flash and stood on a shallow bank, looking back at its companion. At the hunter's second shot, it tumbled over and fell into a nearby channel that had been scored through the earth by flowing rain water. Almost at once, Jim spotted a third tiger running off through the undergrowth at the edge of the grassy patch. As it emerged in a clearing, he let off a shot in its direction and had the satisfaction of seeing it tumble over. Just as the hunter was beginning to feel relieved and satisfied at having dispatched the tigers (which surely included the man-eater) so soon after his arrival, the third animal—apparently dead— started sliding down the grassy slope, coming to a halt only when it hit a small tree and draped itself over it, as it were, with its head and rear portion hanging on either side of it. While Corbett and his companions were enjoying a well-deserved smoke, the tiger started slipping off the tree and fell through the air and down the cliff side. Corbett did not miss the chance to get in a shot as the animal, just before it crashed through the trees and undergrowth crowding the foot of the cliff.

For the next couple of days the hunter followed the man-eater's spoor along the crest of the ridge around a rockslide, alert to the clues it had left on the way and to the alarm calls of kakar, langur and birds. But his luck was out, for the man-eater seemed to have vanished. The following day, 11 April, was also spent in tracking the tigress as it moved from cover to cover, down a ravine and up a slope. The care and caution that Corbett had to exercise in following it is obvious from the seven long hours it took him, on one occasion, to cover a distance of six kilometres. The constant pain in his infected ear, together with the sleepless nights, had sapped Corbett's physical strength and eroded his courage and self-confidence. He realized that he could not sustain his pursuit of the man-eater indefinitely and resolved to make one last Herculean effort to shoot it. So, on that moonlit night of 11 April, he bade his helpers goodbye and instructed them to return to Nainital if he was not back the following evening.

Only those who have spent nights out in the heart of the jungle—albeit in the safety of a forest rest house veranda or high up on a watchtower—can appreciate the magical beauty of a moonlit forest. The quality of light is almost mystical, quite different from the way those who have never seen it might imagine it to be. The silver moonbeams filtering through the foliage of trees create a chiaroscuro of light and shade, where the black seems as stark as the white is brilliant, united by the intermediate greys that take on a deep-violet tinge. At night, the forest settles into an eerie stillness as though it were waiting for something to happen. Every sibilant rustle of grass, every soft 'plop' of dew sliding off a branch, every sigh of a fallen leaf turning over in a gust of wind appears to acquire some special significance. No flickering flame from a candle or lamp lights your way as your eyes try to fathom its depths. All you have for company is your shadow as it springs up as you walk down a trail, now to your left, now to your right, now before you, your heightened imagination filling your mind with a medley of thoughts. To pursue a tiger at night, when it is in its element and you are woefully out of yours, is hardly any ordinary soul's cup of tea. It would need a man in Corbett's mould to take up the challenge with supreme confidence and attempt to best the animal on its own turf.

In a final attempt to bag the man-eater that was eluding him, Corbett followed a cattle track out of the village. From the alarm calls of sambar and kakar, he could determine when the tigress was on the move, and approximately in which direction it was heading. He reached a stretch of short grass, dotted with clusters of oak trees, and paused for a breather under a tree. A short while later, one of the langurs overhead gave its alarm call and Corbett spotted the tigress as it emerged about ninety metres away at the edge of the clearing and lay down. Although Corbett was fairly used to shooting game at night, he was handicapped by his left eye which was by now almost completely shut because of the swelling caused by the abscess. After about half an hour, the tigress limped off ahead towards the right of the hunter. When it had moved a further fifty metres away, he started to stalk the man-eater, moving from tree to tree for cover and closing in to about forty metres of it by the time it had reached the edge of a ravine. It paused for a while in the shadows, not giving Corbett the chance to get in a shot, and then moved slowly into the ravine. Wanting a shot desperately, Corbett bent over and scampered towards the ravine. He realized, too late, that changing his position was a mistake, for in his weakened condition and with the heavy facial swelling, he developed severe vertigo and somehow managed to climb up a nearby tree, so that the tigress could not attack him while he was unable to defend himself. Almost as soon as he had laid his head on his arms to relieve the pain, the abscess burst and pus and blood poured out of his nose and ear.

Sweet, however, are the uses of adversity. For by the time dawn broke over the forest, the swelling on Corbett's face had subsided appreciably, enabling him to use both his eyes. He climbed down from the tree, returned to the village and fell into a dreamless sleep. After some hours of rest and still half-asleep, he heard a commotion outside his tent and learnt that the tigress had killed several goats at the other end of the village. Soon, Jim and his escort (the son of the man-eater's victim) were going down a cattle track that wound down from a depression between two hillocks near the village. The trail crossed a stream and close by, in a hollow, the duo discovered the kill: three goats. Sending the boy back to ensure his safety, Corbett decided to sit out for the tigress near the hollow in which she had left her kill. The trees nearby were mostly chir pines whose trunks rose straight up from the ground for more than nine metres before branches grew out of them to afford a grip. So Corbett had no choice but to sit against a small boulder in the shadow of a much larger rock which offered him a measure of protection from an ambush from the rear.

It was already mid-afternoon. Time seemed to stand still until some blue Himalayan magpies came upon the kill and were followed soon after by a king vulture, looking impressive with its scarlet head and lappets. The birds had been at the kill for a while, when a kaleej pheasant started calling in alarm. The magpies flew off instantly. Corbett knew that the tigress was approaching and redoubled his caution. This was just as well, for shortly afterwards he spied the tigress coming across the shoulder of a hill that lay beyond the high bank on the far side of the hollow. It was staring directly at him, but he knew that if he remained perfectly still, there was a chance that it might fail to notice him against the background of rock. The man-eater sat down behind a large pine tree, biding its time. Then, a short while later, it took a few steps forward and stood looking down at the goats from the high bank. Taking leisurely aim, Corbett pulled the trigger, only to see dust spurt from the far side of the tigress as it dashed forward and disappeared over the high bank. Had he missed the animal altogether in spite of his careful aim? There was little point in crying over spilt milk and the hunter resolved to follow up immediately. As he wondered which way he should head, he discovered to his dismay that the tigress had left no pug marks on the hard surface of the trail. Then he heard men shouting from the village behind him. Looking back, he realized that the men were gesticulating at him to indicate that he should proceed further down the track. Running down a slope, Jim came upon a trail of blood left by the tigress and was able to follow it up without much trouble. He had gone about 200 metres along the narrow track when he reached a dense patch of undergrowth. Realizing that it was a potential ambush point, the hunter approached it with utmost caution. Step by step he proceeded, scanning the undergrowth ahead, his rifle at the ready, every nerve on edge. Soon, he noticed a movement just ahead of him:

it was the tigress, readying itself for a spring. His first shot, as the animal leapt out of cover, drove through its body and the second broke its neck.

Corbett had shot the man-eating leopard of Rudraprayag in May 1926, putting himself through extreme physical hardship and mental strain for months on end without achieving much success in his quest until that last occasion, when he managed to kill it from his perch on the mango tree at Golabrai. In Talla Des, he was in much closer contact with the man-eater, often catching sight of it, and getting in a shot as well. The hunt had been complicated, however, by Corbett's physical disability which had also undermined his confidence. That despite his handicap he did not hesitate to put his life at risk to rid eastern Kumaon of this wily man-eater, is a tribute to his qualities, both as a shikari and as a man.

In his account of his hunt for the Talla Des man-eater, Corbett mentions Tamali, a village along the north face of the ridge. It is, in all probability, the village of Tamuli that I approached via Champawat in 1998. There are limited approaches to the Sarda from the Tanakpur–Pithoragarh main road, one being from Lohaghat to Pancheswar (an angler's dream, given the abundance of mahseer available in this part of the river) and the other from Champawat to Tamuli. I must confess that more difficult approaches through extensive ghat sections and with lamentable road conditions are impossible to imagine! When I first visited the area, I discovered that the small map provided on the last page of *Man-Eaters of Kumaon* was going to be of little help. I was none the wiser when I talked to the locals, at least in Champawat and Lohaghat. No one really knew about the Thak, Chuka and Kaladhunga that Corbett had written about so extensively in his books. One of the main problems was the fact that most of the forest trails the hunter had explored in his time had fallen into disuse. Moreover, the original landmarks had changed and the people of Champawat and Lohaghat no longer had much truck with the inhabitants of the outlying villages near or along the Sarda gorge. The only clue anybody could provide was that there was indeed a Talla Des to the south-east of Champawat, overlooking the Sarda.

So, one afternoon saw me in a 'share' jeep that covered the route from Champawat to Tamuli, moving east along a part metalled, part fair-weather road which spun its way around ravines, pushed through deep, dark deodar forests, passed steep gorges, along the crests of ridges, and cut through 'old growth' oak, chestnut and rhododendron forests. Villages, mostly a cluster of four or five huts, lay few and far between on the edge of pitifully small patches of terraced fields, punctuated by the typical Kumaoni conical haystacks. It took a good deal of guts, I felt, for people to live so far away from medical facilities, schools and bazaars—the benefits of civilization we take so much for granted. That it took us nearly three hours to cover the thirty kilometres to the point where the jeep would turn around and return speaks volumes about the sorry condition of the road. The ridge, whose flank the jeep had skirted on its way, turned progressively towards the south-east. A short distance beyond the village, the motorable road petered out and I had to follow a forest trail. The sun was dipping westwards and as the minutes passed inexorably, the track lay increasingly in shadow. The evening chill was palpable, and no amount of secretly reassuring myself that the Talla Des man-eater had been killed in Corbett's time and could not possibly materialize in front of me at that moment succeeded in quelling my apprehensions about the unknown and the unexpected. All around me lay fairly dense forests, mainly of oak and chestnut, and had anyone dared ask me to tramp after man-eaters in that area with a .450/400 rifle weighing about six kilograms and even paid me handsomely, I would have told him to have his head examined before bursting into tears at the very prospect of having to do so! I was, therefore, very glad to return to the shelter of the jeep, waiting at the village for passengers for the return journey. Soon, we were on our way back to Champawat, being jolted and jerked around, as the jeep navigated the road. But now it was at least a world I was familiar with.

A third approach to Tamuli lies farther south. This was Corbett's chosen route. About twelve kilometres north-east of Tanakpur, at the foot of a tangle of hills and spurs, lies Thuligad, the main starting point for the steep climb to the Purnagiri temple which is poised on a ridge overlooking the Sarda, running east of it. From Thuligad, the ascent to the Purnagiri shrine, a stretch of some nine kilometres, is serious business, especially the last two kilometres. The climb involves negotiating one's way over a stony, rutted track that twists and turns around ridges and through forest, hugging steep hillsides all the way. A sharp turn left, and a welcome surprise awaits the exhausted traveller—the sight of the high, sheer cliffs of Purnagiri. Beyond them, the hills of Nepal rise almost vertically from the bed of the Sarda that separates them. The surrounding hills and forests have a sombre, forbidding air about them, to the extent that pilgrims to the Purnagiri shrine either tread the path in absolute silence or chatter loudly among themselves, no doubt to keep up their spirits.

Corbett writes about two tracks leading to Kaladhunga village, situated on a spur overlooking the Sarda. One goes up towards the Purnagiri shrine before veering off across the north shoulder of the ridge and moving down again to the river. From here it goes on to Kaladhunga. The total distance covered adds up to about twenty kilometres. This road is no longer in use and the inhabitants of the area were unable to provide any information about it. The other track slopes sharply down to the Sarda near Thuligad and skirts the right bank of the river all along the sheer hillside before travelling another twelve kilometres to Kaladhunga. From what I gathered by speaking to the locals, people still travel occasionally between Kaladhunga village and Thuligad. Nepalese labourers and traders sometimes come down that way, crossing the river in small boats. I wanted to use that route myself, intending to go, if not right up to Kaladhunga then at least to the gorge where Corbett had seen the mysterious lights on the slopes of the ridge across the river while camping on his way to shoot the Talla Des man-eater. Enthused by the thought that I had come close to his major hunting ground, I attempted to follow the same route. In places, the track was so steep and the danger of tumbling down into the waters rushing below so imminent that I was glad to use the convenient excuse of a landslide, which had narrowed the width of the track to about ten centimetres, to turn back and claw my way up through the trees and undergrowth to Thuligad. Far, far below, the Sarda, shimmering in the afternoon sun as it coursed past the hills, flanked by broad sandbanks, seemed to mock at my inability to follow through where Corbett would surely have gone ahead without hesitation.

The Sportsman

It would be wrong to assume that Corbett reserved his superb marksmanship and his experience and skills in jungle craft exclusively for tracking down and shooting man-eaters. He never did fully outgrow his childhood and adolescent love of hunting as a sport. In fact, the experience he gained from his sojourns in the jungle in pursuit of game—partly for the pot and partly for the sheer thrill of the chase—served as the fundamental base of knowledge he would rely on when called upon in his later years to pursue man-eaters. As anyone with even minimal experience of field sports will acknowledge, there is something about the cool, fresh air of early morning, the lengthening shadows of dusk, the pungent smell of cordite and the 'high' generated by nervous excitement that lingers in the bloodstream long after the event. Nevertheless, the exploits with rifle and fishing rod that Corbett has written of, belong to a time, space and context so far removed from our own that a conscious effort is called for to understand them. The task is not made any easier by our belonging to an era in which the pace of life is so frenetic that leisure activities are invariably relegated to the backseat, the fine art of hunting for sport has surrendered to the obsession for easy profit, and environmental disasters in the form of extensive deforestation, silting of watercourses and serious depletion of many species of wildlife, seem imminent. To regard hunting of game as a pastime in this context would be morally—and legally—unacceptable.

The ethos was, of course, significantly different in Corbett's time. In the last quarter of the nineteenth century and during the first two decades of the twentieth, wild pig, porcupine, chital and sambar were regarded as common game. It was a time when even the leopard was considered vermin and shot indiscriminately. The tiger too was widely hunted, as is evident from surviving accounts of shikar in those days. J.W. Best, for example, claims to have shot three tigers in a day in the 1920s while a maharaja is reported to have bagged more than a thousand in his lifetime! At the time, the Wildlife Preservation Act (1972), which now regulates and, in certain cases, prohibits the capture or killing of scheduled game in India, was nowhere on the horizon. Nonetheless, a certain degree of control used to be exercised through the issue of game licences, the official booking of forest blocks for shoots and a widely accepted practice of 'open' and 'closed' seasons for shooting game, be it birds or animals. Not that this unwritten rule was not flouted by poachers who were a menace even in those days as they shot considerable game without an official licence. Interestingly, even Corbett's mentor, Kunwar Singh, belonged to that breed.

The difference lay in poachers of that era stalking game on foot, nurturing a healthy respect for the forest guard patrolling the reserve forests over which the forest department exercised jurisdiction and managed according to well-defined plans, and generally using muzzle-loaders or single-shot guns and rifles. Moreover, they usually shot game for food, rarely for the purpose of trade.

It is therefore hardly surprising that a man like Corbett, born and brought up in those times and in a place like Kaladhungi, bordering the terai, its jungles and grasslands teeming with game, should have spontaneously taken up the fishing rod and the hunting rifle. In those days, it was expected that a boy should not only be interested in such outdoor sports and be well able to fend for himself in the forest, but also bring home the occasional fish, fowl or game for dinner. Thus, with the arms at his disposal, starting with the muzzle-loader given to him by his cousin, Stephen Dease, to help him collect bird specimens, and the .450 Martini Henry rifle that the drill master of his school in Nainital had loaned him to the old army rifle he had subsequently bought for fifty rupees Corbett was able to indulge his passion for shooting game right up to his last days in India. He also played an active part, if not the lead role, in organizing and supervising shoots for both friends and dignitaries.

It would not, perhaps, be out of place at this point to give a brief description of the terrain that Corbett covered in fifty years while trophy hunting or shooting game for a meal. It is at Kaladhungi that the spurs running down westwards from the hills below Nainital come closest to the Haldwani–Ramnagar road. Eastwards, towards Lamachaur and farther on to Haldwani, the road lies at a considerable distance from the foothills. Strangely enough, shortly after the road passes Kaladhungi, the landscape flattens out once more for a nearly thirty-two-kilometre stretch in the direction of Ramnagar before the woods and hills make a reappearance near the Sitabani forests, where a causeway spans the river Dabka. The road from Kaladhungi to Nainital runs up the left bank of the Boar, while the Kota road starts from the Boar bridge and goes through rough country on the right bank of the river. After cutting through nearly six kilometres of fairly dense forest, this road arrives at a plateau, where the land these days is given over to cultivation. Cutting across it for another fourteen kilometres or so, the road ends at Kotabag on the banks of the Dabka. Kota has developed into a busy town, surrounded by extensive farmlands, and has a population of anywhere between 15,000 and 20,000. Old residents do, however, remember the vast tracts of forest that stretched across this area in the first two decades of the twentieth century. They also recall how it took them the better part of a day, riding sturdy hill ponies, to reach Kaladhungi. Before the Public Works Department road reaches Kotabag, another one branches off to the west, right up to Powalgarh, seven kilometres away, while a section of it circles back to the Kaladhungi–Ramnagar road at Belparao. West of the Kota road are large expanses of sal and mixed forest through which a track runs towards Powalgarh.

Jim was barely ten years old when he took his first shot at big game. In those days, Kaladhungi was surrounded by forest; it still is, though mostly to the east and north of the village. The Boar flows down from the hills of Nainital, flanked on either side by spurs, ridges and ravines clad in deep forest. The road from Kaladhungi to Kotabag runs along the right shoulder of the river, turning westwards through a short ghat section towards Kota and then farther on to Powalgarh. In the last quarter of the nineteenth century, the forests in that area (which Corbett called the 'Farm Yard'), enclosed by the Boar on one side and the Kota road on the other, were rich in game, ranging from jungle fowl to tigers. Even to this day, the slopes leading down to the river have a fairly dense cover of mixed forests, while large stretches of sal are visible on the upper reaches of the hillside.

On the momentous occasion of his first shoot, Corbett had been hoping to bag a bird for the family cooking pot with the .450 Martini Henry, a most unlikely weapon for a ten-year-old. He had been stalking some peafowl, when he caught sight of a leopard bounding down the slope, evidently disturbed by something it had spotted on the road. As the animal reached the edge of the ravine across which Jim was standing and turned to look back, he shot it in the chest. It was, he realized later, a dangerously risky shot, for the wounded leopard might well have landed on him! Luckily for Jim, the animal leapt over his head and disappeared down the slope. Anxious to bag his trophy, Jim followed the trail of blood down the hillside, past clusters of boulders and clumps of trees, until he noticed the leopard's hind leg protruding from behind a rock. He stalked the animal cautiously and put a second bullet through it as it turned its head to look at him. Trembling with shock and delight, Corbett pulled the leopard away from the blood that was oozing from its body and attempted, at first, to carry it home himself. When this proved too taxing for his ten-year-old frame, he ran four kilometres to his home to ask for help. Along with the helpers who accompanied him back to the spot where he had left the leopard, came Maggie, who was, undoubtedly, proud of her younger brother's achievement.

It is difficult to imagine a ten-year-old of today being given free run of the forest in the area and summoning the courage to shoot a leopard the way Jim did. And perhaps, it is just as well, for despite all the development that has taken place around it, the region is still home to big cats. On a recent visit to Kotabag, a local man described to me how the priest of a small Shiva temple that stood by the road was frozen into silence during his prayers as he watched a tiger saunter past. On another occasion, while walking down the Kotabag road late one afternoon, we were startled by a volley of alarm calls—'Powk, powk, powk!'—from a herd of chital, possibly at some predator in the forested slope to our right.

A considerably older Corbett, out hunting big game, describes an intriguing hunting episode at Devidhura which involved his pursuit of what he refers to as the 'temple tiger'. This was not one of his infamous man-eaters, but an animal that had earned some notoriety by killing livestock. Although this incident took place around 1910, when he was hunting the Panar man-eater, an account of which is given in an earlier chapter, Corbett only wrote about it much later in *The Temple Tiger and More Man-Eaters of Kumaon*, published in 1954. The hunter had come to hear about this tiger and its activities from the priest at the Birehi Devi temple in Devidhura. As mentioned in an earlier chapter, Devidhura is situated between Champawat and Almora. This road roughly follows an east–west direction over a ridge with relatively gentle ghat sections. The slopes fall away to valleys to the north and south. To the north lies a ridge overlooking the Panar, while, far away, the horizon is resplendent with the snowy peaks of the Himalaya. Although Devidhura has developed into a small town, having come a long way from the wilderness it used to be in Corbett's time, the temple is still poised between some massive rocks and faces a huge deodar tree, just the way he described it. You have to squeeze and crawl your way between the rocks to approach the inner temple. Having arrived in Devidhura on the basis of incorrect information he had received about a man killed by the Panar leopard in the vicinity, Corbett decided that his time would be well spent if he went out and shot a sambar that would bring in some meat, both for his own men and for the villagers. So, guided by one of the men from the village and armed with the brand new .275 Wesley Richards rifle he had bought from Manton's in Calcutta, he trekked down southwards from Devidhura. Soon, he came upon a hut near which a tiger had killed a cow. What followed can be best described as a comedy of errors. Corbett tracked the tiger, a large male, for several days. However, as luck would have it, the animal kept appearing at the wrong places and at the wrong moments. Although Corbett was given a chance to try for a shot, he missed his target because he was not yet completely familiar with a particular mechanism of the new rifle. Another time, his helpers accidentally left behind the special cartridges that went with the heavy rifle they were carrying for the hunter. To his credit, Corbett took it all in his stride. He was only thirty-five at the time and hoped that the tiger would live long enough for him to bag it.

છ

The tiger Jim really sought as a trophy, however, was the 'Bachelor' of Powalgarh. He would have to wait until 1930—twenty long years from the time he had gone after the 'temple tiger'—before he could turn his mind to the 'Bachelor' (an account of the hunt is given by him in *Man-Eaters of Kumaon*). Corbett has described in his inimitable style his first encounter with the tiger he fondly refers to as the 'Bachelor'. It took place near a ravine, about four kilometres from his home in Kaladhungi. Why he should have chosen that name for it when the animal was at least ten years old and had, in all likelihood, mated with more than one tigress by then, remains something of a mystery. It was in a spacious clearing, roughly rectangular in shape, with a stream running through it, that the tiger first appeared before Corbett. It crossed the clearing at a leisurely pace, approached the stream to lap at the water, then called a couple of times before disappearing into the forest beyond.

During winter that same year, the *dak* peon who delivered mail from village to village came to Corbett with reports of pug marks left apparently by a very large tiger near a forest track about three kilometres from the hunter's home. Early the next morning, Corbett followed up this lead with Robin, who served as his guide and companion. It seems from the details provided by him that the valley and the foothills down to which they tracked the tiger lay near the Boar, no more than a two-hour trek from Corbett's home. He chose, however, to return home for breakfast and make his way back to the spot, armed this time with his .450 rifle. Not far off, he discovered a buffalo herder in a state of extreme panic, perched on the upper branches of a tree. The herder recounted how the tiger had suddenly appeared and started to growl at him, while he tried in vain to drive it away by shouting at it. While the herder rounded up his buffaloes, Corbett covered him with his rifle and escorted him part of the way to his village so that the man could reach it safely. By then it was already late afternoon.

While the hunter was taking a breather, he heard the tiger call from the direction of some scrub jungle about a kilometre away. Having decided to attract it by mimicking its call, he ran up a cattle track leading in the direction of the scrub jungle, climbed a tree and simulated the call of a tiger. The tiger responded almost at once. Corbett climbed down from the tree and ran back to his original position on a flat stretch of land, calling as he went. The tiger was approaching rapidly and, not finding a suitable tree to clamber up, Corbett lay flat on the ground, half-hidden in the grass, about twenty metres from where the path entered the scrub. He could see some way down the path and was waiting for the tiger to appear along it when he sensed a movement slightly to his right, about nine metres away. It was the 'Bachelor'. As the tiger's huge head emerged from among the bushes, Jim swung his rifle to the right and fired a shot at a point just below its right eye. Corbett writes that he nearly died of fright subsequently, as the tiger, instead of dropping dead as he thought it would, fell over backwards and attacked a small tree with great ferocity, roaring and snarling for all it was worth. Corbett remained prostrate on the ground for about half an hour, too afraid to move, until the animal's roars had died down and the violent movements behind the tree had ceased.

The hunter then crept away but returned to the scene during the next couple of days, trying at first to track the tiger with the assistance of some men, then enlisting the help of a herder and his buffaloes to flush out the wounded animal. But he was obviously out of luck. On the third day, however, he had gone out alone when he spotted the tiger's pug marks on a damp patch along the trail. He followed it cautiously down to a dry stream bed. As he looked around, he noticed the hind leg of a tiger protruding from behind a tree. He could not be sure, however, whether the animal concealed there was the wounded 'Bachelor' or not and was forced to hold his fire. After a while the animal moved away and on approaching the tree Corbett realized that it had, indeed, been the wounded tiger. As he moved towards a stream, wondering where the tiger might have gone, a sambar belled in alarm to his left. Shortly afterwards, the hunter heard a stick snap about forty-five metres away, quite close to the spot from which the sambar had called.

Less conscientious hunters would perhaps have abandoned the hunt at this stage, but Corbett had a wounded tiger on his conscience, and that too the 'Bachelor'. So he carried on, moving carefully through a thicket of small trees with his rifle in position to take care of possible contingencies. Suddenly, he caught a glimpse of something red between the trees. Crouching down, Corbett crept nearly a couple of metres forward, till he could make out the tiger lying on its belly and looking at him. Two shots, one after the other, completed the job and the 'Bachelor' rolled over without a sound. A much-coveted trophy for many hunters, between 1920 and 1930, the tiger had fallen to Corbett's luck and skill. It was brought home, with Robin as escort, and when measured was found to be 3.17 metres over the curves or approximately three metres between pegs. By then, Jim was already well into wildlife photography and he had a snapshot taken with the 'Bachelor' sprawled at his feet, right at the foot of the old kanju tree that still stands to the right of the gate of his house in Kaladhungi.

ℛ

His third hunt for a trophy was that of the Pipal Pani tiger. The hunter had first come across this animal when it was hardly over a year old near a stream the locals around Kaladhungi referred to as Pipal Pani. The next time Corbett saw the tiger, it was almost full-grown and was boldly approaching a chital kill. The hunter frightened it off by firing a shot close to its head, so that it would learn to approach a kill with greater caution, an indispensable lesson in survival.

About three years later, the same tiger would be fired upon by a local landlord while approaching a kill. A day after it was wounded in this manner, the tiger was seen limping through Kaladhungi village, right past the PWD bungalow (which lies close to the left bank of the Boar) and crossing a bridge that spans the canal before seeking refuge in an empty godown. Disturbed by the excited villagers, however, it left the godown, passed Corbett's bungalow at the junction of the Nainital–Kaladhungi and Haldwani–Ramnagar roads, and paused for rest on the outskirts of the village. It remained there for a few days and fed on a bullock that had died of natural causes. Then recovering, somehow, from its wound, the tiger took to cattle-lifting, exacting a toll on the local livestock which the villagers generally let loose to graze on fields adjoining the nearby forests.

The Pipal Pani tiger would carry on in this manner for another ten years or so, growing very substantially in size—as cattle-lifters usually do—and attracting the covetous eye of quite a few hunters. Then, on a winter night, a villager, mistaking it for a marauding wild pig, fired upon it. Hearing of this incident, Corbett scoured the strip of forest between the Boar canal and the foothills for several days trying in vain to catch sight of the animal. Shortly afterwards, he came across a couple of villagers in a tearing hurry to leave the forest. They informed him that a tiger had been calling at the foot of the hills and had caused their herd of cattle to stampede. Asking one of the villagers to lead him to the spot, Corbett came to a shallow depression along the Pipal Pani stream. A tree stood at one end of this depression. Corbett decided to sit up on its branches and imitate the call of a tiger to lure his quarry out into the clearing. His first call was instantly answered from a distance he judged to be about 500 metres away. Then one call followed the other. After about half an hour, when the sun was about to set, the tiger appeared along a path that ran through the depression. Resorting to 'an old device', as Corbett puts it without specifying what it was (I strongly suspect it was a low call or a whistle), he managed to bring the animal up short, and as it looked up he placed a bullet in its chest. So perished the Pipal Pani tiger, very close to the stream near which it had been born almost fifteen years earlier. Corbett's satisfaction at having bagged a trophy that measured about three metres between the pegs was tinged by an element of sadness at the thought that the tiger's call would no longer be heard in the forests around the foothills of Kumaon.

&

Corbett has included the stories of other hunting events in his accounts of shoots targeting one man-eater or the other. Consider, for instance, the shoots that took place in the Rudrapur maidan in 'The Chuka Man-Eater' or the one at Bindukhera (where he suffered a ear injury) that preceded his quest for the Talla Des man-eater. Dr Chris Mills of the Natural History Museum, London, was kind enough to screen for my benefit one of Corbett's films, shot between 1934 and 1935, recording just such a hunting event. It shows a forest in the terai and a line-up of about ten elephants, with the help of which the hunters go on to bag several hog deer, a couple of large swamp deer stags and a leopard. (Copies of these films are also available with the registrar of the Wildlife Institute of India at Chandarbani, Dehra Dun.) Once, in Nainital, I had scrambled up to one of the storerooms on the roof of Gurney House and seen for myself the three leopard skulls, the tiger skull, the four pairs of chital stag horns and the large pair of horns belonging to a swamp deer that Corbett had preserved as trophies.

In *Jungle Lore*, Corbett has also written about the shoots he organized between 1943 and 1945 for the viceroy, Lord Linlithgow, near Kaladhungi—according to Deb-ban, around the 'Farm Yard' and in the forests along the Kota road. Then there was the drive he arranged on his own for the Maharaja of Jind who was keen on bagging an elusive tiger. Corbett had also shot more than one leopard, either because they had killed the bait he had specially laid out for a man-eater or carried off a villager's cattle. As for his passion for fishing in the Himalayan streams, it shines through, both in his story 'The Fish of My Dreams' from *Man-Eaters of Kumaon* and in his memorable account in *The Man-Eating Leopard of Rudraprayag* of the day he spent fishing in the Alaknanda. There were, in fact, times he devoted up to ten days to fishing, indulging in one of his favourite pastimes all the way up the Sarda, the Nandhour or the Ladhya, on his way to some area where the particular man-eater he was commissioned to shoot was operating.

To regard Corbett as an implacable slayer of man-eaters, focussed on his one and only goal of liberating his fellowmen from the depredations of ferocious predators, would therefore be only a half-truth, apart from offering a very one-dimensional portrait of a man who had many interesting facets to his personality. Given the milieu in which he was nurtured, it is hardly surprising that Corbett enjoyed hunting and angling as sports and took obvious pride, like his fellow hunters, in bagging a coveted trophy, be it an oversized tiger or fish, recording the event for posterity on film when he could, as in the case of the 'Bachelor' of Powalgarh. His fans are free to look up to him as a larger-than-life icon. But it would only be fair to Corbett's memory to bear in mind the other very human side of his persona: the enthusiastic sportsman and ardent lover of wildlife for whom duty and diligence had its own time and place.

Jim's Public Face

Most of what we can put down about Corbett with any degree of certainty are gleanings from his writings, be they letters, a meagre collection of his articles (assiduously put together by Kala and Booth) or his own books, six in all. It is indeed surprising that so few from among the dozen or more he knew quite well, including William Ibbotson, Malcolm Hailey, Maurice Hallet and Lord Linlithgow, not to mention friends and acquaintances like Lionel Fortesque and Robert Bellairs (whom Corbett had helped to some extent) as well as some of his Indian friends and neighbours, had deemed it fit to write about him at all. It was only a few among the many he had known in India and helped who took the trouble, when Corbett passed away in 1955, of writing a few lines to the *Times*, London, and to other newspapers as footnotes to his obituaries.

It was not as if Corbett had never been in the public eye. He had been awarded the Kaiser-i-Hind medal in 1928 and the Order of the British Empire, followed by the Commander of the Indian Empire in the 1940s. Both Geoffrey Cumberledge and R.E. Hawkins of OUP,

India, had known Corbett. Yet their writings on him are surprisingly sketchy. It is a pity that this should be the fate of a writer whose first book, *Man-Eaters of Kumaon*, sold more than half a million copies (an impressive number in those days) within two years of its publication. Maggie, true to the last, had dictated some notes on Jim to Ruby Beyts during the very last stage of her life. Fortunately for us, Kala has been able to reproduce them in his book; they fill in some of the missing information about the Corbetts' family life and provide some biographical details about Jim. But they contribute little to a better understanding of the man himself.

There is more to Corbett than meets the casual eye. We are, of course, more familiar with the hunter's public face, thanks to his documentation in *My India* of his days as a trans-shipment contractor in the railways. Both his acumen as an organizer of men and his concern for his workmen become transparent in these writings. Why he chose the railways as a career may be of some interest to those who have only known of Corbett as a hunter. Jim's father had died when he was just six and by the time he had completed ten years of schooling, his eldest brother, Tom, was already married and the family was in need of additional financial resources. With his high-school education, Jim could not hope to join the civil service. The choices left to him as a third-generation Englishman domiciled in India were limited. He could join the army, the police, the postal service (which Tom had joined) or the railways. What remains something of a mystery is how the eighteen year-old

Corbett came to take up a job as a fuel inspector with the Bengal and North-Western Railways (corresponding roughly to the present North-Eastern Railways zone of the Indian Railways), which had its headquarters at Gorakhpur and its local headquarters at Samastipur, 900 kilometres from his home in Nainital.

The initial eighteen months of work required Corbett to supervise the cutting of trees from the local forests allotted to the railways for use as locomotive fuel. This meant staying far from town and on his own. Apart from the devastating impact that such activity must have had on the environment (Corbett, who would later contribute much to wildlife conservation, records that during this period he had cleared close to 14,000 cubic metres of timber), it made for a lonely life, spent outdoors, 'under canvas'. His moments of solitude were devoted to befriending the young of animals and birds and he even adopted some of them as pets. Among these were peafowl chicks, partridges, baby hare and a couple of four-horned antelopes. Strange as it may appear in the context of his later antipathy to snakes, Jim even allowed Rex, a baby python, to share his tent.

Although there was a fair amount of game in the forests around him, Jim was too busy with his work during the day to go out for a shoot. It was usually on moonlit nights, when the faint light had to suffice for training his rifle on a chosen target, that he could do so. These experiences would, no doubt, teach Corbett all he needed to learn about shooting in the dark, a skill that would come in handy when he went after the Talla Des man-eater.

By the end of those eighteen-odd months, the locomotives had started using coal rather than wood as fuel and Corbett had to surrender his post as fuel inspector and adapt himself to different positions in the railways. The following year saw him move from one post to another—that of assistant stationmaster, storekeeper and fuel consumption inspector among others. Then, around March 1896, he was offered the work of a trans-shipment inspector at Mokameh Ghat. Judging by the trauma underlying my own trips to Darjeeling with my parents in the 1950s involving the broad-gauge–steamer–metre-gauge routine, that too as a mere passenger, it couldn't have been an easy job for Corbett, what with having to supervise loading and unloading of goods from the metre-gauge trains to the broad-gauge ones. But he put himself to the task at hand with his usual determination.

Corbett has written at some length and with considerable feeling about these experiences in *My India*. One cannot help but comment on the young man's almost military attention to detail as he organized his workmen. The caste composition of the labour gangs Jim chose to handle the trans-shipment of goods and different types of cargo and his judicious use of Hindus and Muslims to supervise the work and keep accounts were remarkable in a person not yet twenty-one years old. It is apparent from the details provided in *My India* that his income at the time was nothing to write home about. Yet, part of it went towards the upkeep of the family establishment in Nainital. In the course of time, however, Corbett would be earning a fairly handsome income, amounting to nearly Rs 1000 a month—not a small sum at all at the turn of the nineteenth century!

Besides easing his family's immediate financial problems, the railways made a man of Corbett. The responsibility of supervising the work of so many must have been daunting. But with his integrity and sense of justice, Jim managed by leading from the front and sharing the trials and tribulations of his staff. The work also brought Jim face to face with the harsh realities of Indian life—pestilence and disease, rural indebtedness, the practice of bonded labour and the trials of belonging to a low caste—all of which he described with great sensitivity in *My India*. These experiences were instrumental in shaping Corbett's feelings about India and particularly about its rural poor. Despite the hard work, Jim could still muster sufficient enthusiasm to rope in his colleague, Tom Kelly, and his assistant, Ram Saran, to organize Christmas parties for the workmen and their children and even set up a school for the latter, complete with sports teams.

Jim and Kelly also went out hunting for bar-headed and grey-lag geese, travelling several miles towards the end of a winter day on the trolley car allotted to Kelly, right up to the point where a number of village tanks stood along the Ganga. Corbett writes in 'Life at Mokameh Ghat', that they would set out on these excursions when the moon was nearly full so as to get some light to shoot by, much as Jim had done earlier, during his days as a fuel inspector. The geese would come in hundreds, flying low overhead and, as Jim puts it, it took quite a bit of practise to get the proper lead with the shot and to cope with the evasive action the birds inevitably resorted to after the initial shots had been fired. Corbett especially remembered these occasions as some of the happiest he had spent at Mokameh.

I can well appreciate his sentiments, for they were not so very different from my own when I had gone for a similar shoot on a wintry day on the Ganga near Sultanganj, somewhere between Bhagalpur and Munger, more than thirty years ago. We had spent the night in the home of one of the landlords in the area and were hauled out of bed much before dawn by our host's sons who were to escort us for the shoot. To say that the dawn was chilly would be an understatement. With thick blankets supplementing our gear—coats, mufflers, woollen caps and gloves—we boarded the country boats that would take us along the banks and sandpits of the river. In the early morning, as we took up our positions, the geese and ducks were leaving the village fields and tanks and coming down to the sandbanks for the day; just the opposite of what they did in the evenings, the time Corbett chose to go for his shoots. Which outdoorsman could ever forget the honking of the bar-headed geese and the call of the Brahminy ducks as they fly in—the former in long skeins and the latter in twos and threes—and the swish and whirr of the wings as they come in low overhead? But these birds had been shot at before and would quickly try to gain height or veer off sharply, before any gun could be brought to bear on them. In spite of camouflaging ourselves with blankets and drifting down the slow-moving river—just keeping one person on the lookout, peering from beneath the blanket—we managed to get just two ducks for the pot. Luckily, floating down the Ganga in country boats, with the chilly wind whipping our faces and a picnic lunch awaiting us, was just as pleasurable an experience.

During the years Jim spent at Mokameh, there was much else that he did. Apart from taking leave to visit his mother and sisters at Nainital and Kaladhungi, he would go out to hunt man-eaters on request from the government and supervise the work of running his hardware business and his real estate agency in Nainital. He had also volunteered for service during World War I and had led a contingent of Kumaonis in the Labour Corps to assist the war effort in Europe. On his return, he was detailed to go for a short while on combat duty to Waziristan in the North-Western Frontier Province. Apart from supervising the operations of the tea garden he had acquired after World War I near Berinag, Corbett was also running the coffee plantation in East Africa that he had bought jointly with Sir Percy Wyndham. His work with the municipal board in Nainital and his supervision of the affairs of Chhota Haldwani were additional responsibilities. This was a full life by any token and ought to have been sufficient material for an interested biographer. Some of these aspects of Corbett's life are, however, a matter of public record and have been covered by previous writers.

When Jim finally gave up the railways trans-shipment job in 1918 he was over forty-two years old. Little did he anticipate then that the next twenty years would mark a phase in his life when he would be called upon to shoot many more man-eating tigers and leopards and thus bring relief and succour to the people of Kumaon.

If Corbett has any claim on public memory, it is, firstly, because of his relentless pursuit of man-eaters, often at grave risk to life and limb. His second claim lies, of course, in the delectable stories he wrote for the reading public which have stood the test of time.

There are, however, aspects of Corbett's life that those who have written about him have not dealt with in adequate detail. Several of them emerge during a careful study of the hunter's own writings. Consider his formidable stamina, for instance. Despite my own experience in my younger days of walking for miles over hill and dale, with little to sustain me but a few biscuits and a small bottle of water, I never ceased to be amazed by accounts of Corbett's prodigious feats of physical endurance. F.W. Champion, author of the well-known *With a Camera in Tigerland*, is honest enough to admit that he could just about stay on a machan for three days before coming down with a fever. J.W. Best and the late R.C.V.P. Noronha, who had also gone after man-eaters, did not have to stalk them over long periods of time the way Jim did.

Corbett's first passing reference to his physical stamina occurs in 'The Champawat Man-Eater'. In the story he casually lets out that on the first day of the hunt he walked twenty-seven kilometres to Dhari. The return journey of 121 kilometres to Nainital took him two days, part of it completed, of course, on horseback.

He adds that he managed the second leg of the journey, from Devidhura to Nainital, a distance of seventy-two kilometres, by nightfall—that is, in one day. In 'The Chowgarh Tigers', he mentions without much ado that sixteen kilometres under 'favourable' conditions would constitute a comfortable walk of about two and a half hours. That works out to about six kilometres per hour, a speed approximately forty to fifty per cent higher than that achieved by anybody walking on a level road, and not the steep inclines you have to navigate in the Kumaon hills. As any trekker in the foothills of the Himalaya will testify, doing twelve to fourteen kilometres in a day is pretty good going. It should also be borne in mind that on the many occasions that Corbett walked the hills, he was usually carrying his trusty .450/400 rifle, which weighed six kilograms!

In the same story, the hunter writes about his exploration of the valleys and ravines near Dalkania. On hearing that a couple of tigers had been calling in the area, Corbett had followed up the trail of a cow they had killed. Coming up against the tigers in a ravine, he had shot the man-eater's sub-adult female cub. Then, forced to sit up on a tree overnight to ensure his safety, Corbett had been drenched by a sudden shower. By the time he reached a village in the locality the following morning, he had been without a proper meal for nearly sixty-four hours. It was not the first time either that he had followed such rigorous regimens. In his account of the hunt for the Panar man-eater in 1910, Corbett writes about how he had to survive on wild berries for twenty-four hours, an ironical contrast to Sterndale's account in *Seonee* of the sumptuous repast hunters of the time usually enjoyed when out on a shoot: omelettes, khichdi, dry curries, cold corned beef, potted wild ducks' eggs, toast and chapattis. This, however, was a mundane meal compared to what J. Forsyth, another wanderer of the central Indian highlands, feasted on: roast haunch of venison and fillets of nilgai veal, washed down with drafts of claret and Madeira!

Perhaps the most strenuous hunt that Corbett ever went on involved the man-eating leopard of Rudraprayag: it took him ten weeks during 1925 and three months in 1926 to track down and kill the animal. For days and months on end he had pursued the man-eater before bagging him, trying one tactic after another, following trails up and down hills, spending night after night in haystacks, on machans, atop the towers of the suspension bridge—for twenty nights on end, on one occasion—and then sitting up for ten consecutive nights on a mango tree in the village of Golabrai. The other epic hunt was, of course, for the Talla Des man-eater. As we have already seen, in acute pain from a burst eardrum, with an abscess forming inside his ear, Corbett had spent about ten days (including an unforgettable moonlit night that is likely to remain enshrined forever in hunting lore and literature) tracking the tiger in extremely difficult terrain.

To appreciate the significance of these details, one would do well to understand the background: as a child, Corbett had suffered a severe bout of pneumonia and repeated attacks of malaria (which he mentions in his stories about the Panar and Chuka man-eaters). So, it was certainly something more than mere physical stamina that had seen him through his trysts with life-threatening danger. Endurance has just as much to do with mental fortitude and sheer will power, and Corbett certainly had these qualities in abundant measure. His formidable powers of endurance, to my mind, fairly approximate that demonstrated by some of the world's most acclaimed mountaineering heroes, as they scaled and conquered peaks in the Alps or the Himalaya.

For the better part of his active life, practically up to the late 1930s, Corbett was a hunter in the true sense of the term, with his love for shooting and trophy hunting. In the 1920s he had shot extensively in East Africa with Sir Percy. However, the most notable records of his trophy shikar are his stories describing the shooting of the 'Bachelor' of Powalgarh and the Pipal Pani tiger, both cattle-killers and much sought after by the sportsmen of the day. The 'Bachelor' was accounted for in 1930 and Corbett notes with the pride of a seasoned hunter that the tiger measured just over three metres over the curves, almost three centimetres more than the estimate given by Wyndham's trackers some seven years earlier. With the Pipal Pani tiger as well, Corbett records his pleasure at having bagged a trophy that measured 3.1 metres over the curves. In 'Robin', a story he devotes to his faithful pet, the hunter relates an incident involving the shooting of a leopard. During the hunt for the Chowgarh tigers, he went after a bear with the local villagers and killed it with a blow of an axe, shot a large leopard that had killed some cattle, a pair of tigers that had made a buffalo kill and a couple of leopards that had killed one of the buffalo baits.

He had gone on several long shoots after World War I: one with Bellairs to an area near the Trisul peak and another in 1918 to Kashmir for hangul (red deer) with Fortesque. He has written with feeling about the organized shoots for big and small game on elephant-back in Bindukhera and Rudrapur. In fact, as mentioned in an earlier chapter, he himself had organized shoots for the Maharaja of Jind and later, for the viceroy, Lord Linlithgow, just before World War II. *Jungle Lore* is replete with stories of his pursuit of leopards. In fact, when Corbett shot his last tiger near Kaladhungi around the end of 1945, he is supposed to have justified it by noting that the animal had killed some cattle and a horse in the locality, and might have proven in the course of time to be a menace to the villagers.

Both Kala and Booth have dwelt on Corbett's efforts at creating awareness about conservation of wildlife and on his contribution towards setting up the Hailey National Park (later renamed after the hunter himself) where the Government of India launched its Project Tiger in April 1973. If one goes by what Corbett has written about his own exploits, his interest in wildlife conservation and the joys of 'shooting' with a camera instead of a rifle, developed rather late in his career, after reading Champion's book on the subject published in 1927. In the book, Champion relied mostly on flash photography with a fixed camera and flash, operated by a tripwire drawn across game paths. Of course, some pictures were also taken with a hand-held camera, usually while Champion was on elephant-back. It must be remembered, however, that he was no professional photographer and had to find time for this pursuit between his official duties with the forest department. Moreover, the bulky and cumbersome camera equipment of those days was not too convenient for those wishing to pursue the hobby. In fact, Corbett echoed the sentiments expressed much earlier by Champion in his book—that photography of big game presented as much of a challenge as hunting with weapons, because it required just as much patience, skill and the knowledge of animal behaviour as regular hunting, and provided the same thrills without a drop of blood being shed. Thus, between 1927 and 1935, Corbett derived his pleasure from both rifle and camera. The 16-mm Bell & Howell movie camera he subsequently used was reportedly given to him as a gift in 1928 by Lord Strathcona to supplement his favourite .275 Rigby and .450/400 double-barrelled rifles. In fact, he records in 'The Bachelor of Powalgarh', tongue firmly in cheek, that a herdsman whose buffalo had been terrorized by the big tiger, requested him to put aside his camera for the time being and to take up the rifle against the cattle-killer. However, Corbett appears to have been less skilled with the camera than with the rifle. In spite of many opportunities to film tigers in the wild, his pictures suffered greatly from incorrect exposure and focus. Besides, no measures were taken to ensure proper maintenance of whatever he had filmed. As a result, a good number of his films were destroyed by fungus and damp.

It was only after many years of effort and with the

kind cooperation and assistance of Dr Chris Mills of the Natural History Museum in Kensington, London, that I was able to view some of the wildlife films shot by Corbett and preserved in the library. At present, the museum has in its archives five of the hunter's films; three were shot in India and two in East Africa. I watched a couple from the former category; the first ran for about twenty minutes and depicted the famous sequence of five tigers approaching a kill (described by Corbett in the chapter 'Just Tigers' in *Man-Eaters of Kumaon*). The sequence opens with one of his helpers setting up a machan, apparently near a stream bed strewn with boulders, using lopped branches to camouflage it. The watercourse is, in all probability, the Boar itself. A steep hill rises from the opposite bank. The buffalo kill—obviously a bait—is tied to the exposed roots of a large sal tree by the stream. The tigers approach it, one at a time, making their way through lantana thickets down a game track that hugs the hill opposite. The rest of the film shows the tigers approaching and moving behind the lantana bushes to lie down, except for one which is bold enough to cross the stream for a closer look at the machan! Judging by the angle from which the scene has been filmed, it seems that the machan had been erected fairly close to the ground: the approaching tiger is almost at eye level! While some of the tigers in the film are quite large, others are less impressive in size, suggesting that a couple of tigresses had come to the kill accompanied by semi-adult cubs.

While this particular film was obviously shot near a

bhabar stream, the second one, of around twelve minutes' duration, is clearly set in the terai with its characteristic topographical features: streams bordered by sandbanks or clayey soil running through extensive grasslands. The film shows a hunting party of about a dozen men and women, complete with sola topee and hunting jackets, setting out on elephant-back from a tented camp on a clear morning. The presence of several liveried attendants on the scene suggests that the group included a number of dignitaries. The hunters are shown crossing streams on elephant-back and picking up a couple of large barasinga (*Cervus duvauceli duvauceli*) stags in hard horn, a pair of hog deer and, finally, a leopard. Compared to the first film, this one is more competently shot, in terms of both exposure and camera movement. Corbett's third film features Kumaoni women in traditional attire and is not relevant for the purposes of this book.

Although Kala quotes the Reverend A.G. Atkins, then pastor of the Union Church in Nainital, as having been told by Corbett that the latter's 'conversion' from hunter to wildlife conservationist was triggered by his revulsion at the indiscriminate shooting of waterfowl by some hunters, the records do not suggest an overnight change. It is true that by 1931 Corbett was turning away from shikar and becoming actively involved in photography (clearly a surrogate for hunting with a rifle) and conservation issues. It is also a fact that he became an honorary secretary of the Association for Preservation of Game in Uttar Pradesh. It must be noted, nonetheless, that this body was affiliated to the All India Sportsmen's

Brotherhood, a name which says it all! But by 1932, Corbett had devoted himself to writing about conservation problems. He began with an article on the Pipal Pani tiger, published in the *Hoghunters' Annual*, 1931. The second piece came out in the *Review of the Week*, published from Nainital, in 1932. For the first time, Jim explicitly acknowledged that while watching a tigress and her cubs feeding on a sambar kill, he had experienced no feelings of regret for not having taken a shot at them. He also highlighted the problems posed by poaching, especially over salt licks and waterholes, and by the indiscriminate issue of gun licences. Corbett had begun to speak out, moreover, on the issue of 'balance of nature'. Here again, he seemed to be echoing the views expressed by Champion in his book, where the latter mentions how predators maintain the balance of nature by hunting down prey like deer and pig. Without carnivores keeping their numbers in check, these animals would become a menace as far as forest plantations and village cultivation were concerned. It may be recalled that Jim had also corresponded with S.H. Prater, who had been on the editorial board of the journal of the Bombay Natural History Society since 1923 and wrote introductions to several articles on the preservation of wildlife published in the journal in 1932–33. Some of Prater's ideas may also have influenced Corbett.

Since 1935 or 1936 Corbett was giving lectures in Nainital and elsewhere to create awareness about the importance of conservation. It was Mrs Kiran Verma who informed me when I met her in the course of my research that Corbett had given talks on the subject, between 1940 and 1942, at her alma mater, the All Saints' School in Nainital. She recalls that these lecture-demonstrations were usually organized between July and August, when the students had settled in for the semester following the long winter vacation. Corbett would arrive late in the afternoon, carrying his walking stick and clad in his customary white half-sleeved shirt, khaki shorts and knee-length socks. He was affectionate towards the children, singling them out sometimes by addressing each child as 'My boy' or 'My child'. Usually, the talk was preceded by a film, apparently now lost, of a mongoose catching a snake, followed by magic lantern pictures of chital, sambar and other animals including, naturally, the tiger. The talks, which lasted between an hour and an hour and a half, offered illuminating insights into animal behaviour.

In the meantime, the measures initiated by E.A. Smythies and other forest officers like him (with Corbett's sound advice and able support) to have the Patli Dun area in the Ramganga valley declared a sanctuary, bore fruit. In 1934 it was declared a protected area and the first official national park in the country was named after Sir Malcolm Hailey. It has subsequently been renamed Corbett National Park.

Corbett's real contribution to the conservation effort in India lay in writing about wildlife and sharing his love of the jungle with his readers. It is clear from the books he wrote about the Indian jungles in the foothills of Kumaon that an intimate understanding of and passion for a subject can make it transcend mundane perception and lend it that rare poignancy which captures the imagination of millions of readers. Consider the detail into which Corbett delves, borrowing from his vast fount of knowledge, as he advises us on how to approach a tiger in the wild without being detected. He shares Champion's conviction that tigers have no sense of smell and tells us how they stalk their prey upwind (that is, against the direction in which the wind is blowing) by factoring in the instinctive awareness of a herbivore's highly-developed sense of smell and ambush it as it moves downwind. Conversely, Corbett suggests that a hunter should be watchful of his downwind side if walking upwind during a stalk. Moreover, he perceptively points out how, during the day, the wind tends to blow uphill in the Kumaon hills, reversing its direction when dusk falls.

Corbett also tells us how important it is to study the pug marks that tigers leave on the track or on tree trunks while frequenting a trail, often observed in national parks like Dudhwa, Ranthambhor and Corbett and, as I have discovered for myself, in unprotected areas as well, like the one I travelled through during an afternoon trek from Chorgalia towards Haira Khan. These pug marks, writes Corbett, offer a number of clues (as they did during the pursuit of the Mohan man-eater) regarding the sex of the animal, the direction in which it was travelling when it passed through the area and other vital information. Years later, these details would come in handy for those in charge of India's Project Tiger to carry out the periodic census of tigers in national parks and sanctuaries.

Apart from wind direction and tracks, Corbett relied

a great deal on the calls of birds, monkeys and deer to locate tigers and leopards. The intonation and frequency of their calls and their behaviour patterns often provided Corbett with valuable clues during his shoots. He knew, for instance, that jungle crows, vultures and yellow-billed blue magpies sometimes approached a tiger or leopard kill to pick up whatever scraps of flesh they could manage and their behaviour would often indicate whether a tiger was in the vicinity. Moreover, if a tiger or leopard left its kill out in the open without having been disturbed while feeding on it, it suggested that the animal was not likely to return to it. In addition, kaleej pheasants, white-capped laughing thrushes, scimitar babblers and jungle fowl often called out in alarm if disturbed by a carnivore and usually fluttered off, thereby alerting the hunter.

Despite the range of his knowledge, Corbett had to be infinitely patient during a stalk. In his story on Robin, for instance, the hunter reveals that he was so cautious while using some chital to stalk a wounded leopard that it had taken him nearly an hour to cover a distance of just fifty-five metres. Again, while pursuing the Talla Des man-eater, he had managed to cover a mere six kilometres in seven hours. His classic description of a stalk is given in *The Man-Eating Leopard of Rudraprayag*, where he tells us how he stalked the hangul alone by exploiting the animal's natural curiosity.

In *Jungle Lore*, Corbett has preserved for posterity the precious nuggets of information mined from his experience of the Indian jungles. Distilled within the pages of the book are his observations of seventy years of wildlife in the jungles of Kumaon, a veritable primer for future generations of wildlife enthusiasts in India. It was on the sands of the dry nullah bed in the forests across the aqueduct behind Arundel that he had received his first lessons in differentiating between the tracks left by kakar, barking deer, chital, sambar, wild pigs, porcupines, bears, tigers and leopards. It was just as important to find out how long ago the tracks had been made and in which direction the animal had been travelling. It was Corbett alone, among the many writers on game hunting in India, who specifically recorded the finer details of reading the Book of Nature, absorbing the information either written in the sand or carried on the wind, drawing valuable inferences from it and making it a part of his second nature.

ॐ

Needless to say, it is mostly because of his books that people have come to know about him. His books are also the reason why he lives on in their memory. Here was a person who, by his own admission, had had just ten years of schooling. He had attended no courses in creative writing either. On the contrary, he had busied himself with different professional activities, none of them even remotely literary. Yet, he had found the time to write articles, compile some of his stories of the Indian jungles in an anthology, *Jungle Stories*, and privately publish them sometime between 1934 and 1935. According to a message sent by Corbett to his American publishers (quoted by Booth in his book), he was pushed into this decision by Lady Violet Haig, wife of the then governor of the United Provinces. By the time Corbett started writing, a great many books on big game and small game hunting in India had already been written by Sanderson, Sterndale, Forsyth, Champion, A.I.R. Glasford, Engles, A.W. Wardrop, C.H. Stockley and others. What was it, then, that lent Corbett's writings their uniqueness and everlasting appeal?

Corbett had taken to writing in the 1930s when he was in his late fifties. At this time, he had a reasonable income without having to slog for it and some spare time on his hands. The first articles, highlighting some of the conservation issues of the day, were unremarkable, but competently-written essays. They contained the seeds of the elements that would germinate in his later and better-known books. The first and most important of these elements was what is often called, in audio-visual media parlance, an 'establishing visual'. The opening lines or 'shots' fixed the time and setting of the narrative in just a sentence or two. From this point onwards, it was the natural development of the main story in hand.

The tale of the Pipal Pani tiger—Jim's very first attempt to put his thoughts and experiences into writing—takes the reader straight away through a ravine that pierces into the foothills to the scene where the hunter, alerted by the alarm call of a chital, discovered for the first time the tracks of the tiger on the sands of a small stream. In the following article, 'Wildlife in the Village: An Appeal', published in 1932 in the *Review of the Week*, Corbett uses his opening lines to place the reader in a small village in the bhabar, that strip of land just below the foothills, with low ridges and shallow valleys, cut through in places by hill streams. This was surrounded by forests and grasslands, but, even with no dearth of game, tigers troubled the villagers. The article goes on to explain how both the nature of the villagers and of the countryside changed irrevocably, bringing death and destruction to the local game. A classic 'establishing visual' is used by Corbett in the opening paragraphs of *The Man-Eating Leopard of Rudraprayag*. Here, he escorts the reader from the dusty plains to Kedarnath, pausing on the way for a dip in the holy Har-ki-Pauri at Hardwar, then moving across the Lachhman Jhula and up the pilgrim road to his destination. The feeling of intimacy that this word-picture generates lends immediacy to the hunter's stories and helps the reader to relate to them in ways no other literary device could equal.

There has also been some speculation over the authorship of Corbett's stories. Had he written them all himself, people wondered, or had he received some help? Rumours abounded for a while that Ibbotson had ghostwritten the stories for his friend—an insult to both men, in my opinion. According to R.E. Hawkins, who had received the manuscript of *Man-Eaters of Kumaon*, from Corbett for the OUP in Mumbai and subsequently liaised with him on a regular basis while editing the text, it was entirely Corbett's work. Kala notes, however, that according to Marjorie Clough, a nurse with the Red Cross whose name is mentioned in one of the early chapters of this book, Maggie had assisted him at every stage of the writing, recalling events and suggesting words or phrases that would best convey his thoughts. This could well be true, for Maggie had been at Jim's side since his childhood, keeping house for him when he was out on shoots, nursing him back to health when he was ill and sharing life's simple pleasures with him at Kaladhungi and Nainital. In fact, Mrs Kiran Verma revealed that Maggie had been a keen birdwatcher herself and had left quite a few pages of notes on her experiences. Could her contribution to her brother's jungle stories have been the reason underlying the use of archaic language ('bestir', 'fickle jade chance' and 'thence', for example, in *The Man-Eating Leopard of Rudraprayag*) in Corbett's books, a feature that is absent from his articles on conservation? Corbett's sister might well have made a significant, if unacknowledged, contribution towards the writing of his books on the Indian jungles, a fact she was more than willing to shield from the public eye. Interestingly, Hawkins himself was keen about natural history and may well have introduced relevant changes in the manuscript.

Apart from the use of terms like '*chhota hazri*', Indian English expressions like 'Don't *ghabrao*' and indigenous words like '*tamasha*' and incorrect spellings for place names, what also characterizes Corbett's storytelling is the tendency to add colour to his tales. That he enhanced his stories on more than one occasion is borne out by the wife of a forest officer serving in Kumaon at the time. Norah Vivian, in her comments to Martin Booth, about a passage written by Corbett in 'The Chowgarh

Tigers', refutes the hunter's claim that she and her husband had missed a chance to shoot the man-eater because they had mistaken it for a bear and held their fire. The same inclination, on Corbett's part, to lend extra flavour to an episode is apparent in the description of the scene where the hunter meets up with the Chowgarh tigress on the bed of a ravine. In the letter he wrote to Maggie (quoted by Booth) after shooting the tigress, the hunter mentions that as he looked over his right shoulder, he had seen the tigress. The animal had, apparently, flattened her ears, opened her mouth and started forward. But by then Corbett had swivelled around and shot her dead. When he writes about the same experience in *Man-Eaters of Kumaon*, however, the details of the incident have been significantly dressed up to stress on the proximity of the tigress (given as 2.4 metres), her expression (as if she were smiling at him in anticipation of the kill) and the slow movement of the rifle, supported by one arm, till it was aimed at the animal and the shot hit home.

Contrary to the illusions people may harbour about Indian jungles and the excitement of hunting for big game, the experience is very much like being on the battlefield—days and months of inaction filled with routine drills at the base, interspersed with short bursts of extreme tension and intense activity. Corbett would spend days and weeks tracking man-eaters without coming up against them. A blow-by-blow account of such hunts would have been tedious for the average reader, a fact the hunter knew only too well and kept in mind when he wrote his books, expunging the bits from his experience that would have been of little interest to the layperson and thereby keeping the reader's interest alive. Among the other devices that he resorted to were, firstly, an anthropomorphic approach that involved referring to an animal as if it were a human being (Corbett calls the tiger a 'large-hearted gentleman', for example) and, secondly, the trick of having the reader accompany him, so to speak, to a particular location, such as the circle of hills resembling an amphitheatre in 'The Champawat Man-Eater'. This enabled him to capture the reader's attention and ensure his involvement in the story. Similar writings, using both devices, may be found in Sterndale's *Seonee*, Jack London's *White Fang* and *Tarka the Otter* by Henry Williamson. They constitute a league of writers on natural history against whom Corbett can surely hold his own.

Yet another device Corbett falls back on is the interpolation of the story with other events such as fishing excursions or bear hunts which serve to break the pace of the narrative, take the reader's mind off the lack of success in bagging the man-eater and retain his interest till the conclusion of the story. Consider the episode involving the Himalayan tahr teaching her kid how to jump down to a narrow ledge in 'The Chuka Man-Eater'. In *The Man-Eating Leopard of Rudraprayag* which describes, perhaps, the longest and most tedious of hunts undertaken by Corbett, the chapter entitled 'Fishing Interlude' serves this purpose very well too. Among the classics of the genre is, of course, 'The Fish of My Dreams' in *Man-Eaters of Kumaon*, where Corbett shares with the reader his unalloyed joy in fishing for mahseer in the hill streams of Kumaon.

Among Corbett's greatest assets as a writer is his canny ability to put the reader's own 'grey cells' to the test, somewhat in the manner in which Agatha Christie's famous detective, Hercule Poirot, takes the reader through his paces in solving a mystery. Leading the reader to an unlikely location in the jungle, Corbett offers him a hint here, a clue there, encouraging him to join the author in a bit of jungle sleuthing. *Jungle Lore* contains the finest pieces of jungle sleuthing ever written about. One such episode involves Corbett's discovery of the tracks of a large male leopard while he is out on a shoot for jungle fowl. He tracks it to a point where he finds that it had lain next to a small depression, obviously interested in something that had caught its attention. A short distance from there he notices the deep hoof marks of a large sambar, and again, some way off, near some trees, traces of blood and a few tufts of sambar hair. Corbett builds up the sequence of events from similar scraps of evidence to demonstrate how the leopard had stalked the sambar doe, leaped on to its back in the course of the attack and retained its hold, despite the deer's efforts to shake it off, even dashing against a tree in the attempt. Another such story is about his outing, one evening, to retrieve a chital kill. On returning home, Corbett discovers that his shoes are covered with a layer of red dust. Any other person would have just brushed it off, washed his feet and gone to bed. Not so Corbett. He ponders over the mystery and is out again the next day trying to solve it. He retraces his footprints, made the previous night, and soon comes upon some loose red earth next to a culvert, churned up on the side of the forest road by cartwheels. He determines from the tracks left in the soft earth that a tiger had lain down close to the culvert to watch him pass. Warned by his sixth sense, it was at this point from which Corbett had veered off the path and moved away from the tiger, thus having to walk through the stretch of red dust.

As any good writer should, Corbett uses pauses or a change in pace of the narrative to recount his story and to create a sense of unease in the reader's mind, thus intensifying interest in what is about to unfold. He refers in more than one place to a sixth sense that warned him of danger while out trailing a man-eater. In each of these accounts, as in 'The Chowgarh Tigers', 'The Mohan Man-Eater' and in *The Man-Eating Leopard of Rudraprayag*, the reader is made to pause and follow Corbett, step by step, as he confronts the danger or it abates on its own. Such instances of a feeling of heightened tension are there in 'The Chowgarh Tigers', where the hunter lies down near an overhanging rock in a ploy to attract the man-eater and when he is stalked while going down a curving cattle track, passing close to a pile of rocks. In 'The Thak Man-Eater', Corbett describes in detail the lay of the land as he decides to catch up with the tigress. These episodes reveal a tautness in Corbett's writings that is sadly missing from the accounts by other writers of hunting and wildlife experiences in Indian jungles.

All said and done, most writers would like their pieces

to 'read well', at a pace which enables the reader to simultaneously absorb and appreciate what is written, without any strenuous effort on his part. This quality is much in evidence in Corbett's books. His felicity of expression in describing a sunset followed by twilight in the Indian jungles or a trek through the foothills of Kumaon, as in the tailpiece to *The Temple Tiger*, emerges from his acute powers of observation, his empathy for his subject and a careful choice of words. As far as the first two qualities are concerned, Corbett is virtually incomparable. With respect to the third, if indeed he was assisted in his writing by Maggie as some have claimed, one can honestly declare that he is well complemented. In writing about wildlife and the poor rural folk of the Kumaon hills, Corbett tried in his own way to bring the lives of the people, the 'salt of the earth', whom he loved into focus. In the process, he has left us a still more precious legacy: a perception and understanding of India, especially of her jungles and wildlife, that we would have been very much poorer without.

The Man Within

Although the Corbett we know from his books appears to be free from most prejudices and inhibitions, it should hardly come as a surprise to anyone that a man born in 1875 would have been considerably influenced by Victorian morals and manners. Conforming to the societal norms of the era involved a strict segregation of the public persona from the private one. Social propriety prevailed over individual desires, and commitment to the family overrode personal convenience. Austerity, an overreaction perhaps to the excesses of the Georgian era that had preceded, prevailed, and it was implicitly believed that sparing the rod would spoil the child. Class distinctions were very firmly entrenched and rarely breached. It was only to be expected that the expatriate community living in India at the time and mainly comprising Englishmen, Irishmen and Scots, would be inclined to abide by the customs and norms laid down by their compatriots in the mother country.

Even this relatively small community was broken up into groups which moved in different social circles.

Those Britishers who were in India for trading or administrative purposes for a specific number of years, on the understanding that they would return 'home' after completing their tenure, were considered a breed apart from their compatriots who had been domiciled in this country for more than one generation and rarely contemplated the possibility of going back. Then there were those who had either 'gone native' or married into the Indian community and were unlikely to ever be accepted again in respectable social circles back home. Apart from the subtle differences in attire that distinguished these separate groups, the careers that they chose also revealed which group they belonged to. Many of those who had come straight out of the British Isles were either in the civil and military services or practised law and medicine. A few held senior positions in the police and in the railways. The domiciled Englishman or Scotsman had little or no chance in terms of either education or influence to make it to Haileybury or Sandhurst and had to content himself, for the most part, with middle-order government posts in the railways, the police, the port and the post and telegraph, among others. Of course, they would all meet in church on Sunday, but they were likely to sit in separate pews. They greeted each other in the street, but preferred the company of their peers when out socializing. It was into this milieu that Jim Corbett was born, the eleventh offspring of Irish parents domiciled in India for three generations.

In the opening paragraphs of *Jungle Lore*, the hunter writes that on several occasions fourteen children (including his siblings and the neighbours' children) would sit around a fire in the middle of an Indian country road, listening to ghost stories narrated with gusto by Dansey. It is evident that domiciled families like the Corbetts and their neighbours usually had several children unlike their true-blue counterparts from England who preferred to raise small families, possibly because their upkeep and education in England cost a great deal of money, even in those days. For the Corbetts and their neighbours, the idea of sitting out on the road by a fire made from sticks collected from the nearby jungle, was not anything out of the ordinary. More so because in the backwaters of Kaladhungi the Corbetts and domiciled families like them could enjoy a relaxed lifestyle, far from the probing eyes and wagging tongues of 'civilized' English society. Young Jim was not only allowed to run barefoot in the jungle, something that the 'proper' expatriate would perhaps have found quite abhorrent, but took local superstitions like the one about the *churail* seriously enough to mention it in *Jungle Lore*. Like many domiciled Britishers, he had also come to appreciate, maybe even accept, certain Hindu customs. He may well have been a frequent visitor to the shrine of Pashani Devi which still stands on Nainital's Thandi Sarak, the way it did in his time. He notes in *The Temple Tiger* that he made the customary offerings at the Birehi Devi shrine at Devidhura. According to people I met at Kaladhungi who had known Corbett when they were children, he often resorted to the familiar Hindi slang '*paji*' (rascal) if he wished to reprimand somebody. Apart from the fact that it would have been quite beneath an Englishman of standing to stoop to such language, Corbett's choice of the word is surprising. For, in a place like Kaladhungi which adjoins Muslim-dominated Moradabad, Rampur, Bajpur and Bareilly, the Urdu equivalent, *badtameez*, was far more likely to have been used.

The hunter also tells us how, around the age of eight, he was expected to escort his sisters and the neighbours' daughters to the nearby canal for a bath, with instructions to warn them if locals from the village approached the canal along the path skirting it while herding cattle or collecting firewood. Jim adds, curiously enough, how *he* too was sternly ordered to look the other way when the girls—aged between nine and eighteen—stepped into the waters of the canal and their cotton dresses, swelling up with the current, billowed over their heads. Perhaps it is in episodes like these that the clue to the never-ending mystery as to why Corbett never married lies. We Indians, curious as always about the quirks of individuals and forever fascinated by behaviour that defies facile explanation, are particularly intrigued about the single status of the healthy and personable Corbett. D.C. Kala suggests that such experiences—he refers to them as 'childhood traumas'—may have had something to do with Corbett's decision to remain a bachelor. It sounds rather implausible to me, though, that this factor could have played so important a role in Jim's decision to remain single. It is quite natural for a child of eight to explore his body and be curious about how it is different from that of the opposite sex. Jim may well have stolen a glance or two at the girls while they were bathing, flouting express instructions not to do so. Moreover, in many Indian villages, members of the opposite sex have often used the same pond to bathe in, though at different times of the day and at separate ghats to ensure privacy, and have gone on to marry and bear children without problems.

It is apparent from Corbett's own writings that he was no prude as far as women were concerned. Writing about the first man-eater he shot in 'The Champawat Tiger', the hunter describes an incident in which some men travelling along the road between Champawat and Dhunaghat had come across the man-eater carrying off a naked woman. Gathering together more people, they had set off to find the victim. Corbett relates how they found the woman, really no more than a young girl, lying naked on a large slab of rock, with the blood licked off her body by the tiger. She looked as though she were asleep and would awaken at any moment, bewildered and ashamed at being touched by strangers. In the same story, he refers to the incident where the tiger had killed a young girl of about sixteen or seventeen. Arriving at the spot of the kill, Corbett had found the blue beads from her broken necklace scattered amid the splashes of blood staining the ground. Her sari, which had been torn off her body by the predator, lay a little way off. Further down, in a pool by a small stream, the hunter had found the girl's leg. The pitiful sight of that shapely limb had haunted him for a long time afterwards. In 'The Chowgarh Tigers', Corbett describes in some detail how the man-eater had attempted to kill a young girl and had torn her garment off her body in the process. In *The Man-Eating Leopard of Rudraprayag*, he offers, yet again, an explicit description of the woman, no more than twenty years old, who had fallen victim to the carnivore in a village near Chhatwapipal. He informs us that she was quite fair and robust in build and that the leopard had torn off all her clothes and licked her clean before feeding a little from both the upper and lower portions of her body. Had the hunter suffered from any inhibitions about the opposite sex, he would, in all likelihood, have avoided such explicit descriptions. Although it is true that he wrote about these episodes as a mature man of sixty-eight or more, the fact remains that Corbett had willingly provided certain details he could well have chosen to obscure or omit, with no one being the wiser.

Kala insists, however, on pursuing his train of thought, even going so far as to suggest that Corbett's phobia about snakes originated from a subconscious desire to suppress the male libido of which the snake is believed to be a symbol. According to him, the hunter's pursuit of man-eaters had something to do with his secret impulse to destroy the element of aggression in the female of our species, an element of which the man-eater is an emblem. His argument seems somewhat far-fetched, for had Corbett not pursued and shot man-eating tigers as well as tigresses like the ones which had preyed on the villagers of Kanda and Mohan? The leopards of Panar and Rudraprayag had also been males. Kala has, however, unearthed an interesting bit of information about a fixed deposit that Corbett had once made out at the Faizabad branch of the Allahabad Bank, in the name of one Aditya Binay Kumari, apparently a member of Uttar Pradesh's well-known Balarampur family. The members of the royal family used to visit Nainital often—a house bearing their name still stands in the hill station—and it is quite natural for Jim to have become acquainted with some of its members. Kala suggests that for an Englishman to have made such a gesture for an Indian woman hints at some kind of a romantic attachment.

The romantic angle has, in fact, intrigued and perplexed other writers on Corbett as well. In his book, *Carpet Sahib*, Martin Booth writes of his hunch about Jim's special feelings for Jean, the wife of his good friend Ibbotson, and has even elaborated on the subject in a personal letter to me. It should be borne in mind, however, that in his story about the Thak man-eater, Corbett is effusive in his praise of Ibbotson. Moreover, his obvious fondness and regard for his friend come through repeatedly in *The Man-Eating Leopard of Rudraprayag*. I feel that in all fairness to Corbett's memory and in the absence of any concrete evidence to justify speculation over whether he was indeed in love with Jean Ibbotson, we should go by his notes alone and infer what we can from them. Booth also writes that after Jim's mother died in 1924, he apparently fell in love with a woman called Helen who was related to one of the forest officers he had known. But the difference in age and social status supposedly put paid to any plans for marriage they might have envisioned.

The real reason behind Jim's bachelorhood was,

probably, the most obvious one: socio-economic. His mother and his two sisters, Eugene Mary Doyle and Margaret Winifred (Maggie), claimed his attention, directly or indirectly. Both Kala and Booth indicate in their books on Corbett that the women were quite possessive about him and in all likelihood were not particularly keen on Jim marrying and leading an independent life. In the expatriate community and Indian society of the time, this would hardly have been regarded as unusual. To sacrifice personal desires for the 'greater good' of the family would have been quite in keeping with the tenets of Victorian tradition to which Jim was evidently no stranger. The responsibility of taking care of an ageing mother and two unmarried sisters was one he was likely to have accepted without much fuss. In return, he could rely on them for tending to his needs and for moral support in good times and bad. That he was keenly aware of their concern for him is clear in the regularity with which he sent telegrams to his mother, and later to Maggie, reporting his safe arrival at his destination whenever he was called away to hunt for a man-eater or with news that the predator in question had been duly accounted for.

The positive aspects of such a relationship are obvious in the loyalty with which Maggie stood by Jim through thick and thin, in sickness and in health, supportive till the last. Still, there may have been times when Jim thought of having a family of his own. In a letter written by Jim to Maggie in May 1920, quoted by Booth in his book, the hunter expresses his sympathy for a friend, Robert Bellairs, who happened to be a bachelor like

him. Jim adds, significantly enough, that Bellairs's fate
was possibly what lay in store for the 'last of the
Mohicans' everywhere. Knowing of his fascination with
Fenimore Cooper's books, one may be forgiven for
assuming that Corbett was probably referring to himself
as well.

Another factor which may have had a bearing on his
marital status was the compulsion, driven by the
straitened financial circumstances of the Corbetts, to
seek a livelihood at the age of eighteen. Jim had to
establish himself before thinking of marriage. Moreover,
the job he was compelled to take up at this stage of his
life with the Bengal and North-Western Railways,
headquartered at Gorakhpur, serving as a fuel inspector
and subsequently, as assistant stationmaster, storekeeper
and fuel consumption inspector, before accepting,
sometime in March 1896, the work of a trans-shipment
inspector at Mokameh Ghat, left him little time for
himself. He was hardly twenty-one years old then and
it is also debatable whether the income he earned during
the early years of his career was enough to support a
family of his own after contributing to his mother's
household in Nainital and meeting his own expenses.

If hard work and the demands of his family had
failed to sublimate Corbett's sexual urges, his love of
the jungle would surely have taken care of any problems
he may have faced on that score. His rambles in the
jungle, deciphering the language of the wild etched by
bird and beast in the sandy beds of forest streams, and
listening to the tales recounted in the whistle and
chuckle of birds, in the hoot and cough of monkeys,

would have been absorbing enough. Add to this passion his fondness for hunting with gun and rifle, for fishing with line and spinner and his growing love for wildlife photography and you have an understanding of the fulfilment that must have been his, albeit of a different kind. Given the context, it is not so difficult to accept that Jim may have come to terms with his bachelorhood without suffering from a sense of resentment or regret.

What must have helped him enormously to endure his solitary life was his positive approach to life. It emerges time and again in his stories, where he handled the fatigue and frustration that followed days and nights of stalking an elusive man-eater by firmly believing that one day he would surely be able to get the better of the animal. Another quality which must have stood Corbett in good stead when he was out stalking and shooting man-eaters was his fine sense of humour. Consider, for instance, the following episode from *The Man-Eating Leopard of Rudraprayag*. Ibbotson, who had accompanied Corbett for the better part of this hunt, had sent a *patwari* (a junior village official) to gather information on a missing person, believed to have been killed by the man-eater. The *patwari* had returned, anxious to be of help, carrying a sketch of the man-eater's pug marks which he had found near the missing person's house. The sketch comprised one perfect large circle in the centre with five equally immaculate smaller circles clustered around it, all traced with a compass! (I may as well add that some of the pug mark tracings collected during the census operations of our own Project Tiger are not all that different from the artistic efforts of the *patwari* in Corbett's time.)

The story which Corbett obviously relished narrating, however, is the one in *Jungle Lore* about Sir Percy Wyndham's efforts to catch a python for the Lucknow zoo. The very idea of an officer of his rank, with the irascible temper to which Sir Percy was prone, getting into a scrape of this kind is outrageous enough. To get on with the story, the commissioner, Corbett and two helpers had entered the jungle on elephant-back and soon spotted a python lying in the shallow waters of a jungle stream. Sir Percy asked his helpers to tie a noose and trap it. They were obviously reluctant to do so, despite his kind offer to cover them with his rifle. Making no headway with his subordinates, Sir Percy appealed to his friend, Corbett, to pitch in and was summarily refused. Exasperated, the commissioner dismounted from the elephant and got down to the business at hand, his helpers in tow, trying to slip a rope under the snake. Engaged in an offensive that relied heavily on the strategy of advance and retreat, the three men were taken unawares when the snake suddenly reared up. With a cry of terror, the assistants thrust the rope into the commissioner's hands and fled. Not to be outdone in the race for his life, Sir Percy also abandoned the rope to its fate, and all three men, united in retreat, splashed through the waters of the stream and disappeared into the forest nearby, while the snake swam off in the opposite direction to nurse its grievances in the shelter of the roots of a tree with overhanging branches, leaving Jim chuckling to himself at the turn of events.

Corbett's humour was, however, directed as much at himself as it was at others. In 'The Chowgarh Tigers', he recalls how during a bear hunt in which he participated, the only way he could keep up with his companion during the walk uphill was to call for frequent halts for no other purpose than to enjoy the view. He also confessed how, during the hunt, he was relieved to notice that the bear was running downhill, when its so-called pursuers were running uphill! Described in *Jungle Lore* is another episode that goes back to his early years as a hunter and involves a forest fire. In his account, Corbett refers with amusement to Kunwar Singh's scandalized reaction to the sight of him wearing shorts. The old poacher who had served as the hunter's guide in the forest had assumed that in his hurry to get ready so early in the morning, Jim had forgotten to wear his trousers! While hunting for the Mohan man-eater, Corbett describes how on coming upon a fallen tree beyond which he suspected the man-eater to be hiding, he was reminded of a cartoon he had seen in *Punch*, where a shikari passing by a large rock looks up and sees a lion looking down at him from the top. The caption below read: 'When you go out looking for a lion, be sure that you want to see him.'

Among the many qualities that Corbett possessed was his heartfelt concern for his fellow human beings. Had Corbett not truly cared for the Indian rural folk he often had to work with, both during his career in the railways and later at Kaladhungi, it would not have been possible for him to write a book like *My India*, shot through from start to finish with an abiding current of concern and consideration. Corbett's concern for his fellow men manifested itself in different ways. To some he provided assistance in kind, like building a stone house for Mothi, one of his tenants in Kaladhungi. To others, he offered financial and moral support, as in the case of Budhu, the bonded labour who came to work for him at Mokameh Ghat, and Lalaji, whom he virtually snatched from the jaws of death after discovering him desperately ill near one of the railway sheds. Both *Jungle Lore* and *My India* are replete with instances of Jim's mother and later Maggie and the hunter himself providing succour to many with shelter and medicines and, failing that, at least a few kind words of sympathy and encouragement. Corbett had developed a genuine empathy for the poor of India, particularly those belonging to Kumaon, the place he regarded as home. This is borne out by his vivid descriptions of the approach to Hardwar and Rishikesh in *The Man-Eating Leopard of Rudraprayag*, his conversation (in 'The Muktesar Man-Eater') with the little girl, Putli, who was taking a bullock to her uncle's house and travelling through the man-eater's territory, unescorted, his story of Mothi and his family, and the tale of Harkwar and Kunthi in *My India*.

At the same time, Jim could be quite high-handed in dealing with these people. Consider, for example, the occasion on which he threatened to burn down a village if the treatment of Kunwar Singh, his old poacher friend from Garuppu, who was suffering from the ill effects of opium addiction, was found wanting in any way. Corbett relates a similar incident in *The Man-Eating*

Leopard of Rudraprayag. He and Ibbotson were on their way back, one night, after a fruitless watch for the man-eater. On the way, the lamp hit a rock and the mantle broke, forcing the two men to approach a hut in pitch darkness. When their knocking on the door failed to produce a response—for most villagers living in that area considered the man-eater to be the devil incarnate and saw no reason to take any chances—Jim threatened to burn down the hut unless they opened the door. Elsewhere in his books, he makes poor Chhota Punwa carry a big rock on his head for quite a distance without offering him any explanations just to teach him a lesson for having carelessly placed Jim's rifle on the sandy bed of a stream. I am also at a loss to understand why, on more than one occasion, Corbett took his time, fishing for as long as ten days along the Nandhour, the Ladhya or the Sarda rivers, to reach the area where a man-eater had been reported, rather than making for his destination post-haste. In any other person, this may well have been condemned as callous and irresponsible behaviour.

Jim's interest in the rural folk inhabiting the areas he was familiar with was paternal rather than that of a peer. This is evident in the personal care he took of the villagers from Kumaon whom he had recruited for the Labour Corps during World War I. It is equally manifest in his tacit approval of what he describes as the 'rough and ready' but always humane administration of justice in 'Pre-Red Tape Days', the story about his tour with Sir Frederic Anderson in *My India*. Corbett conforms, therefore, to that mould of the expatriate in which a

markedly paternalistic, even patronizing attitude was
balanced by the concern of the domiciled Britisher for
the welfare of his long-standing Indian neighbours and
friends. It was this trait in his personality which must
have led him to record—undoubtedly with a measure
of self-importance—in his story, 'The Queen of the
Hills', that the rural folk regarded him as a 'white
sadhu'. The idea is repeated in 'The Chowgarh Tigers',
where he writes that the tall, gaunt man who had
directed Corbett during the bear hunt looks upon him
as a sadhu. In the *The Man-Eating Leopard of
Rudraprayag*, he also writes that the hill people credited
him with supernatural powers. One cannot help
wondering while reading such passages whether Corbett
really did come to believe that he was an ascetic, putting
himself through various forms of austerity, sacrifice
and danger to bring deliverance to a people.

Could the ambivalence of his attitude towards the
rural folk in India, which led him to look upon them
with a mixture of paternalistic concern and the colonial's
condescension, have influenced his decision to leave the
country where he was born and grew up as soon as the
possibility of its independence became inevitable? We
shall never know. After all, a great many of the
expatriate administrators the Corbetts had known and
were close to, had left for other destinations in 1947.
These officials must have had their reasons for doing
so, the primary one being, possibly, their apprehension
that if they stayed on they might be obliged to conform
to the policies laid down by the new government of
independent India and even follow the directives issued

by Indian colleagues in senior positions. Besides, some of Corbett's relations had also emigrated and the sense of security that the cosy circle of domiciled Britishers had once enjoyed in India naturally diminished. By 1947, both Jim and Maggie were beginning to feel the burden of their advancing years, one of their prime concerns being the fate of the remaining sibling, should one of them die. They must have been equally worried about the uncertain law and order situation, given the political turmoil that had surrounded the Quit India movement in 1942 and the communal riots of 1946 and 1947.

Not that political agitation was unknown in the Kumaon region till the 1940s. Strong undercurrents of economic and political movements had swept the area right from the beginning of the twentieth century. In fact, during the last quarter of the nineteenth century, considerable agitation had followed the reservation of forests by the government, culminating in a conference called by Major General Wheeler in 1907, focusing on this issue. Political movements had been organized against the practice of *kuli begar*, the free labour that the colonial administration demanded of the local people, and *kuli bardayash*, the compulsory free provisioning of touring British officials. These movements had led to the formation of the Kumaon Parishad in 1916. Govind Ballabh Pant, who would later become deputy prime minister of India, had led a major agitation in 1919 against the Rowlatt Bill. Har Govind Pant and Chiranjilal headed new movements against *kuli begar* in 1921.

The outcome of the evolving political situation would

have been clear to an intelligent observer like Corbett. It is, therefore, surprising, that while narrating his stories, he should have so effectively insulated his readers from the ever-changing and increasingly volatile political atmosphere in which he lived and worked. Could Corbett's silence over the matter have been a form of denial, stemming from the wishful thinking that the way of life he had loved and enjoyed as a part of the colonial administration would go on forever?

To add insult to injury, the Government of India had decided, following the Partition of the country in 1947, to rehabilitate in parts of the terai region, the families displaced from West Punjab. Corbett had long held this area to be sacrosanct for the forests and wildlife it contained. The fact remains, however, that the forests of the terai and bhabar had been so severely exploited since the beginning of the nineteenth century by both the local populace and the colonial administration that sometime between 1824 and 1825, Bishop Reginald Heber had actually remarked on the extent of the devastation. While it is true that Sir Henry Ramsay, the first commissioner of the terai and bhabar regions, had tried to regulate the exploitation of the forests from 1861 onwards, he had actively encouraged the cultivation of land in the area. Significantly enough, Corbett's father was one of the beneficiaries of that policy. Moreover, from the mid-nineteenth century onwards, smelting of iron had been taken up in Kumaon, first by C. Davies & Co. and then by Macdonald & Co. Both used charcoal made by burning timber collected from the local forests for the purpose (I had, in fact, discovered a couple of such smelters lying just above a nullah, about half a kilometre east of the Corbett Museum and around sixty metres north of the road to Kaladhungi bazaar, right opposite the spot where a school building now stands). Meanwhile, *kham* settlers, brought in from other parts of the state in large numbers by the administration, had cleared tracts of land in the terai which they had turned over to cultivation. Exploitation of the forests in the area had increased with the extension of the railroad to Bareilly and Haldwani and to Moradabad. In 1917, the policy of categorizing the forests as 'reserved', 'protected' and 'panchayati' was formally introduced, considerably restricting their use by the local population, with the discretion in notification and usage vested with the then British forest administration. As was to be expected, this type of administration had both negative and positive consequences.

As a part of that set-up, directly and indirectly, Corbett failed to understand the magnitude of the human tragedy unfolding around him following the Partition. It was quite beyond his comprehension that any government with democratic and humanitarian pretensions would have to respond urgently to the situation at hand if it were to retain a modicum of credibility. Corbett's inability to face up to the political and social realities of his time is betrayed by his remark (as quoted by Booth) to Lord Wavell (Lord Linlithgow's successor as viceroy of India in 1943), that tigers didn't have votes; human beings did. In attempting to balance his concern for the forests and wildlife of Kumaon with his relationship with the villagers of Kaladhungi and his other Indian friends, Corbett seems to have proved himself unequal to the task. One can, however, hardly blame him for being what he was—only too human.

A still more unusual quirk in Jim's personality, which emerges repeatedly in his writings, was his fascination for superstitions and his fondness for interpreting inexplicable events and experiences as manifestations of supernatural phenomena. This aspect of his nature was in direct contradiction to the man he seemed to be in his 'official' capacity: the upright Christian, the dutiful soldier, the well-organized railway trans-shipment contractor who would later become the hard-headed businessman, and the keen observer of man and nature. Although Corbett avers that he had spent too much time alone in the jungle to be a victim of his own imagination, he has admitted elsewhere to being superstitious about snakes and mortally afraid of crossing some of the hill streams in Kumaon because of the pythons lurking in the water. In 'The Kanda Man-Eater' he confesses to being convinced that unless he killed a snake, his efforts to bag the man-eater would be of no avail. In the same story, he relates how he came across a hamadryad or king cobra while walking from one village to the next and stoned it to death, after which he went on to shoot his quarry. In the other hunts that Corbett has written about, he does not specifically mention whether he killed a snake before accounting for the man-eaters. In the story about the Rudraprayag man-eater, however, he does describe a fight at Golabrai between a pair of hoodless cobras and tells us how one of them was beaten to death with a stick by Ibbotson. That same night, Corbett managed to shoot the man-eating leopard. In the story of the Talla Des man-eater, the hunter confesses that he avoided going out on a hunt on Fridays.

Jungle Lore reveals many instances of Corbett's tendency to interpret events that had no logical explanation. He relates how, as a child, he heard the call of the 'banshee' in Kaladhungi while out in a storm and on mustering the courage to investigate the shrieking sound, discovered that it was caused by one fallen tree rubbing against another! Even as an adult, he was ready to give supernatural experiences their due. In *The Temple Tiger*, for example, he failed, for no particular reason, to shoot the animal, even when on three separate occasions the opportunity to bag it was ripe. Then there was his experience with Bala Singh who was apparently 'attacked' by the 'demon' of Trisul, when he was out shooting near the mountain of the same name with Bellairs, shortly after World War I. In yet another story, Corbett tells us of the strange lights he saw in the gorge of the Kali, below the heights of Purnagiri, when he was on his way to shoot the Talla Des man-eater in 1929. He was sufficiently intrigued by the experience to have written at length about it. At the same time, he adopted a scientific attitude and tried to find a logical explanation for what seemed, at first glance, to be inexplicable, as in the case of the banshee, the *churail* and the lights in the gorge.

Still more hair-raising were his experiences while out shooting the Champawat and Thak man-eaters.

Although some contend that the first incident took place at the Champawat forest rest house, this was not the case. Corbett had travelled from Pali to Champawat, twenty-four kilometres to the east. The tehsildar there requested him to move to another bungalow, a further six kilometres away. Obviously, the second place had a bit of a reputation, for instead of staying the night with Corbett in the bungalow, the tehsildar had preferred to cover those six kilometres on foot and return to Champawat, although the sun had set and the area happened to be within the regular beat of the man-eater. Corbett is non-committal about the incident and merely writes that tales of the supernatural have no place in a book about jungle stories. He never does tell us about his experience in the haunted bungalow.

In Thak, the village had already been abandoned because of the depredations of the man-eater and Corbett was aware that the predator might be hiding in any one of the empty huts with their doors ajar. One evening, he decided to sit up on a tree over a buffalo that had been killed by the tiger. The kill lay close to a mango tree that grew near the village. It was here that Corbett had been followed by the man-eater on an earlier occasion. As mentioned in an earlier chapter of this book, it was close to full moon and shortly after evening descended the moon rose, bathing the countryside in silver. Corbett could make out a sambar doe and fawn feeding in a field close by. A little later, a kakar gave its alarm call, indicating that a tiger was about. This was followed, immediately afterwards, by a long-drawn-out scream. It came from the direction of the village and sounded as if it had been wrenched out of a human being in the throes of death. Corbett was as startled by it as the kakar, which stopped calling. The sambar and its young fled from the scene. Later, Corbett would learn from the headman of the village that the agonizing cry, as the hunter had described it, resembled that of a man who had, a few weeks earlier, been dragged off a tree, while he was plucking leaves, and killed by the man-eater.

ß

If there is one feature of Corbett's personality that ardent fans of his books find difficult to pin down, it is his habit of making statements that lead to discrepancies in his stories. In 'The Thak Man-Eater', for example, the hunter's memory seems to play tricks, resulting in confusion about dates. His claim that he had killed the Chuka man-eater six months earlier, is inconsistent with the facts. If we accept that he had killed the Thak man-eater in October 1938, his declaration would automatically place the shooting of the Chuka man-eater in April 1938. Yet, Corbett had actually shot this man-eater the previous year, in April 1937. Similarly, in *The Man-Eating Leopard of Rudraprayag*, the hunter informs us, at one point, that he had sat up for twenty nights on one of the towers of the suspension bridge. Elsewhere, in the same story, he changes the number of nights to twenty-eight. In 'The Thak Man-Eater', he mentions in passing that he had shot three man-eaters in the same region, a few years ago. Yet, the only tigers he specifically refers to in the story are the Chuka and Talla Des man-eaters; the Thak man-eater about which he was then writing, could not be counted as the third. Again, in 'The Thak Man-Eater', he wrote that he had come to the end of his stories about the jungle and about tiger shooting. But in 1947 and in 1954 respectively, he went on to offer, to the obvious delight of his admirers, *The Man-Eating Leopard of Rudraprayag* and *The Temple Tiger*. In 'The Champawat Man-Eater', Corbett mentions that on some occasions he had camouflaged himself, draping a sari around his body in the way hill women usually did, before cutting leaves from a tree—a ploy to disarm the man-eater and lure it closer. It is, however, only in 'The Chowgarh Tigers' that he indirectly writes of having done so only on one occasion.

Apart from these jarring discrepancies which might be attributed to oversight or an unreliable memory, readers must contend with Corbett's curious propensity for preferring innuendo and suggestion to directness, as in his account in 'The Talla Des Man-Eater' of an incident that took place in the grasslands of Bindukhera in 1929. A large hunting party, of which the hunter was also a member, was organizing a beat with seventeen elephants. The hunters had already shot some florican, peafowl and a hog deer when, as Corbett puts it, a high-velocity rifle accidentally went off near his left ear, severely damaging the eardrum. It is not as if such hunting accidents were rare. What intrigues us, though, is Corbett's way of referring to it as an accident and, at the same time, appealing to the 'Recording

Angel' to avert his gaze from it. It immediately piques the reader's curiosity and makes him wonder whether this was, indeed, a mishap or something more deliberate. A couple of paragraphs later, when the hunter refers to the incident, he calls it an 'accident' within quotation marks, heightening the mystery and the reader's suspicions and adds that he has not raised the subject with the intention of eliciting our sympathy. Yet, he refrains from further elucidation. He goes on to tell us how he left the next morning in great pain on the pretext of having work to do back home and, with some justfication, pleads with the 'Recording Angel' to look the other way. His infirmity would have an important bearing on his experience of shooting the Talla Des man-eater, for hearing is one of the most indispensable faculties when out shooting in a jungle and Corbett's hearing had been seriously impaired because of his burst eardrum. He rounds off his account with the remark that had his other ear been in normal working order, the consequences of the accident would have mattered little. But the truth was that his other ear had also been affected, some years back, by an 'accident' with a gun. Once again, the quotation marks are Corbett's. He tells us later, though, that medical treatment did succeed in partially restoring his hearing.

Curiously enough, elsewhere in his writings we discover that long after the accident that had caused such extensive damage to his eardrum, the hunter was able to pick up minute forest sounds. In 'The Bachelor of Powalgarh', for instance, he was capable of hearing the tiger call over a kilometre away, that too a year after the accident had occurred. In the concluding part of the story about the same hunt, he describes how he hears, from a distance of about forty-five metres, the crack of a branch underfoot, as if a heavy animal had just lain down. He goes on to stalk the tiger and shoot it. In the tale of 'The Thak Man-Eater', which he shot in 1938, he is able to hear the tigress call from across a valley, and then decides to call out the animal to shoot it. I am yet to figure out what Corbett had hoped to gain by laying more emphasis on his disability than it warranted, unless it was to lend colour to his stories and enhance their appeal. His reticence about the mishap which caused damage to his eardrum could well have stemmed from his attempt to protect the person responsible for it.

ॐ

Like most human beings, Corbett was a man of many parts. Overbearing at times, though only on rare occasions, he was kind and considerate towards most. This does not necessarily mean that he had a charitable bent of mind. His genuine concern for the welfare of underprivileged Indians was coloured by a patronizing attitude towards them. In this respect, at least, Corbett's thinking and behaviour were not so very different from that of his fellow expatriates. He could not, after all, help being a product of that culture and era. Reserved, yet far from unsociable, Corbett resembled, in certain ways, the tiger he often hunted: his friends were few in number, but he shared abiding bonds with them. Not given to expressing himself verbally, he compensated for this lack by translating his thoughts into the written word and his inborn sense of humour lent his prose and his personality that extra warmth, as his letters, articles and books testify. It is to the hunter's credit that despite his colonial 'handicap', he cared enough about his adoptive country to gain invaluable insights into its beliefs, customs and traditions. They were instrumental in helping him develop a rare empathy for the common people of India that few, burdened with his legacy of domicile, could have been capable of. It was a quality that would endear him to those who knew him and enrich his tales of the Indian jungles for those who never would.

The Final Salute

Like any other person, famous or obscure, Corbett ought to be accepted the way he was—a man of admirable qualities with some very human failings. It would seem from the observations on his character outlined in these pages that despite the Corbetts having been domiciled in India for three generations, King and the Old Country remained something of a lodestar for Jim. For all his concern for the poor and humble folk of India, he could not regard them as self-sufficient individuals with minds of their own. Moreover, the hint of the colonial in him prevented Corbett from acknowledging India as a country inching towards self-rule. Whether this blind spot was ingrained in him or had been borrowed from men like Sir Frederic Anderson and Sir Percy Wyndham or acquired during his career in the railways when he had to fend for himself and learn to assert his authority, cannot be determined with any certainty. That he should, nonetheless, have decided in 1947 to leave for East Africa, expressing doubts as to whether there would be anybody at all left in India to bury Maggie and him when they died, is a sad reflection on his diminishing faith in his long-time friends and neighbours.

It is possible that advancing age and declining health—Corbett was seventy-two years old at the time of India's independence—may have aggravated the hunter's anxieties over this issue. Some are of the opinion that Maggie was reluctant to leave India, but surrendered to her brother's will. According to Kiran Verma, however, it was Maggie who had insisted on leaving India. She had apparently persuaded Jim to accompany her by raising the issue of the difficulties their mother faced at the time of the Sepoy Mutiny in 1857 and of her own apprehensions about the reports filtering in, during 1946, of looting and rape. The siblings, especially Maggie, rued their decision in their later years. It is possible that *My India* (published in 1955), with its outpouring of feelings and concern about this country, was written by Jim as an act of expiation.

In October 2004 I got the opportunity to visit Nyeri, close to the Aberdare Mountains in Kenya (about 150 kilometres north of Nairobi), and I made it a point to visit the place where Jim had been buried. This is 'coffee country', with a rolling countryside which rather reminded me of Meghalaya. Almost in the centre of the town is the Anglican Church of St Peter's, and in the adjoining graveyard Jim's gravestone is set off by colourful bougainvillea. I reflected, wistfully, that it had been a long journey for Corbett from the hills of Kumaon to the slopes of the Aberdares, as indeed it had been for me.

As for myself, the image of Corbett as demigod that

I had worshipped as a child, did lose some of its gloss when I explored his books with a critical eye and scrutinized the articles and notes published by Booth and Kala. Once he had stepped down from his pedestal as it were, the hunter became more approachable in my eyes and infinitely more human.

In the final analysis, he stands tall and far above many on at least two counts. I salute him as much for the supreme naturalist he was at a time when environmental awareness was not a priority, as for the engaging manner in which he wrote about his experiences in the Indian jungles, making them come alive in a way that few—if any—can match. Apart from the incomparable reading pleasure his books have given me, his words of wisdom about the jungle and its denizens have inspired many like me to become passionately interested in wildlife and to discover the jungles for themselves.

ଛ

Those who have enjoyed reading Corbett's books the way I did and are keen to pursue their interest in him might consider visiting Haldwani or Tanakpur. The Baramdeo or Brahmadeo barrage is about three kilometres from Tanakpur. Golden-finned mahseer may still be found near the barrage over the Sarda. About fifteen kilometres from Tanakpur, and accessible by 'share' jeep, lies Thuligad. Located at the foot of the Purnagiri hills, it nestles amid stretches of sal and verdant mixed forests. Close to where the Water Works

office stands today, a trail leads down the steep hillside
to the Sarda. In Corbett's time, the tramline laid down
by Collier ran along the river and the hunter had kept
to it on his way to shoot the Talla Des man-eater. The
route has now fallen into disuse and one would require
the help of porters and guides to make it to Chuka,
about thirty kilometres away, in one piece. The
alternative route along the Sarda to Chuka, Thak and
Kaladhungi requires you to travel beyond Sukhidang
on the Tanakur–Champawat road. You must get off at
the Chalthi bridge and take the rough forest road,
overgrown with vegetation, that runs past the iron
cantilever bridge along the south or right bank of the
Ladhya as it courses towards the Sarda. This route is
recommended only for those travelling in a group,
accompanied by porters and guides, for the trail cuts
through dense forest and the going is tough. The ideal
time to use this route is after January or February,
when the forest road is likely to have undergone repairs
and is used by the occasional timber-loaded truck.

If you are keen to follow the route that Corbett had
described in 'The Thak Man-Eater', a bus is available
from both Haldwani and Tanakpur (the journey involves
a wide detour these days) to Chorgalia, where deep in
the heart of the jungle stands a beautiful forest rest
house with the Nandhour flowing past. Apart from its
natural splendour, the area's claim to fame is the man-
eating tiger which is reported to have visited it some
twenty years ago. More than thirty kilometres away,
up along a jungle track that crosses the river in several
places, is Durga Pipal. From there, you can make your

way to Chalthi on the Tanakpur–Champawat road and catch up with the forest road that runs along the banks of the Ladhya, right up to the Chuka and Thak villages. Since this route traverses dense jungle and is a good thirty-five kilometres from Durga Pipal village, it is best to travel with an escort of local people and porters.

If, on the other hand, you get off at Haldwani's busy railway station, the series of high ridges running east to west from below Nainital right up to Bhimtal will tower over you, with wisps of fog still clinging to the treetops. If you have the time, take a quick peek at the north-west corner of the Haldwani interstate bus stand. The building that stands there, resembling a small bungalow with a colonnaded veranda, is the telegraph office from which Jim had received and sent many of his telegrams. It was here that he had spoken, some sixty years back, to Hugh Stable, military secretary to the viceroy, Lord Linlithgow, about the latter's proposed visit to Kaladhungi. Right next to the Haldwani bus stand is the Base Hospital (now known as the Sobha Singh Jina Hospital), mentioned in several of Corbett's stories. With its large portico, long verandas and arched doorways, the building is representative of typical colonial architecture. From the stand, buses ply regularly to Nainital, Bhimtal and Dhanachuli (from where you have to transfer to a 'share' jeep heading for Khanshio and the Kala Agar ridge, the backdrop for Corbett's story about the Chowgarh tigers).

Nainital is a couple of hours away by bus. As you walk down the Mall, past the rows of shops and up a short stretch of road on the right, you will come across a stone hall opposite the Nainital Club. A neat structure with a small portico in front, it is now known as Shailley Bhavan, the new avatar of the erstwhile Chalet Theatre, where Corbett first learnt about the Rudraprayag man-eater and where the Nainital Amateur Drama Society used to stage occasional plays. Across the Mall is the Boat Club to which Corbett was denied admission for years, as the membership was then open exclusively to high-ranking British officials. Close by, overlooking the lake, is the round bandstand that Corbett had built for the people of Nainital. Further down, at the water's edge, is the Naina Devi temple which Corbett used to visit. Across the 'Flats' to the right rises the municipal office building with its clock tower, where Jim served as a councillor for several years. The rather grand towered and buttressed building that sits midway up the slope above the municipal offices now serves as the Nainital bench of the Uttaranchal high court.

Some distance up and to the left, on a small knoll, stands the church of St John-in-the-Wilderness, where Jim was christened and his parents were buried. Now open to the public only on Sunday afternoons, the stone church has fine stained-glass windows depicting scenes from the Bible. The cemetery to the south of the church contains graves bearing the names of some interesting individuals: Rivers Carnac, possibly related to a famous general in the British army, and Col. William Garstin, related to John Garstin, the architect of the Town Hall in Calcutta, among others.

At a higher elevation and more to the left stands Gurney House, looking rather lost among the oak and chestnut trees. If you are fortunate enough to meet Mr P.K. Verma, its present owner, or even members of his family, they would gladly show you around the house where Corbett lived for so many years. Apart from the chair cover in the drawing room, embroidered by none other than Maggie, the furniture includes the sideboard built by Jim in his Mokameh days and the old table and chairs the Corbetts once used. They are still kept in the dining room the way they used to be in Corbett's time. The head of a ghoral and that of a sambar are displayed in the foyer along with other trophies (possibly from East Africa). A rambler rose climbs up the east-facing bay window. If you close your eyes, you can almost conjure up Maggie and Jim having their afternoon tea next to it.

Right next to the church, opposite the tourist lodge near Sukhatal, is the bus stand. From here, you can board a bus heading for Ramnagar and Bajpur and retrace the route Corbett had used many, many times when making the journey from his winter home at Kaladhungi to Nainital. The road runs past Khurpatal before cutting through a good expanse of forest to meet the Haldwani–Ramnagar road at Kaladhungi. In Corbett's time, the road to Ramnagar did not exist and he has written of taking the train from Haldwani, via Kashipur, to reach the place. Close to the junction and right next to the Corbett Museum stands the tea shop owned by Deb-ban Goswami, son of Bara Punvan and grandson of Dhanwan, whose name crops up in Corbett's account of a near-fatal incident with a wild boar. Over seventy years old now, Deb-ban is one of the few people still living in Kaladhungi who have met Corbett. He had even been taught the alphabet by Maggie. Listen to him reminisce about those days over a cup of tea.

At Deb-ban's tea shop, you might even find a guide to accompany and direct you as you trace the route from the forest bungalow to the bridge which the Pipal Pani tiger crossed, down the stone-paved canal and then along a dry nullah at the point where the Bijli Dant aqueduct is located. Arundel, the Corbetts' first home which had survived up to the early 1990s, has vanished without a trace. To the right of the iron gate, leading into the Corbett Museum, is the kanju tree before which the hunter had himself photographed with his trophy, the 'Bachelor' of Powalgarh. If you walk about a kilometre in the direction of the Kaladhungi bazaar, you will come across a culvert over a nullah opposite the Saraswati Children's School. A short distance up the nullah lie the derelict kilns where iron used to be smelted in the days of Sir Henry Ramsay.

A little time and inclination is all you need to take a walk in the direction of Kotabag, down the road that takes off to the right, just beyond the bridge that spans the Boar. From a vantage point on the hillside, the Boar appears like a ribbon of shimmering water. Corbett called the stretch of jungle lying between the river and the road the 'Farm Yard' and it was here that he roamed and shot game for more than fifty years. If you are reasonably lucky while exploring the area on your own, you will hear the call of peacock and jungle fowl, chital and kakar. A further four kilometres up, the forest road, once just a fire line, veers off to the left towards Powalgarh, twelve kilometres away.

A fairly frequent bus service covers the twenty-nine kilometres that separate Kaladhungi from Ramnagar. Garjia is five kilometres from Ramnagar, while Mohan lies a further nineteen kilometres ahead. Buses ply regularly between all these points. From Mohan, the road going left towards Morchula leads to a ridge a couple of kilometres away. It was to the east of this point that the Mohan man-eater asserted his territorial rights. Somewhere in between, and eighteen kilometres from Ramnagar, is the Dhangari check post. If your papers are in order, you can move on to Dhikala, some thirty kilometres ahead, with its grand vista of the Ramganga and the Patli Dun valley. Beyond this point stands the Kanda ridge.

En route you can pause for a while at High Banks, where the Ramganga narrows to no more than eighteen metres, and watch the mahseer slip-streaming in the powerful current. If it is springtime, the simul and coral trees will be in bloom and the orioles, parakeets, hair-crested drongos, chloropsis and barbets will be busy fluttering around the flowers. Having perhaps explored Thuligad, Chorgalia, Nainital and Kaladhungi on the way, you could pause a while beside a sal grove, listening to the murmur of leaves and the distant call of the chital. And as you inhale the aroma of the sun-drenched earth under your feet, you are likely to feel, as I did, that it had been worth the while, after all, to have 'tracked' Jim and thus come to know a little more intimately a man you've admired from afar and the land that he had come to love.

Bibliography

Best, J.W., *Forest Life in India*, London: John Murray, 1935

Booth, Martin, *Carpet Sahib*, London: Constable & Co., 1986

Carrington Turner, J.F., *Man-Eaters and Memories*, London: Robert Hale, 1959

Champion, F.C., *The Jungle in Sunlight and Shadow*, Dehradun: Nataraj Publishers, reprint, 1996

————, *With a Camera in Tigerland*, Dehradun: Nataraj Publishers, reprint, 1994

Corbett, Jim, *Man-Eaters of Kumaon*, London: Oxford University Press, 1944

————, *The Man-Eating Leopard of Rudraprayag*, London: Oxford University Press, 1947

————, *Jungle Lore*, London: Oxford University Press, 1953

————, *The Temple Tiger and More Man-Eaters of Kumaon*, London: Oxford University Press, 1954

————, *My India*, London: Oxford University Press, 1955

Hawkins, R.E., *Jim Corbett's India*, New Delhi: Oxford University Press, 1980

Johnsingh, A.J.T. and G.S. Rawat, *On Corbett's Trail*, The Oxford Anthology of Indian Wildlife, vol. 1, ed. Mahesh Rangarajan, New Delhi: Oxford University Press, 1999

Joshi, Maheshwar P. 'Kumaun: Archeological and Historical Perspective', in *Kumaun: Land and People*, ed. K.S. Valdiya, Nainital: Gyanodaya Prakashan, 1988

Kala, D.C., *Jim Corbett of Kumaon*, New Delhi: Ankur Publishing House, 1979

Mittal, A.K., 'Kumaun during Gorkha and British Rule', in *Kumaun: Land and People*, ed. K.S. Valdiya, Nainital: Gyanodaya Prakashan, 1988

Mohan, Dhananjai, 'Trekking through the Sharada Valley', in the newsletter of the Wildlife Institute of India, vol. IV, 2003

Noronha, R.C.V.P., *Animals and Other Animals*, Delhi: Sanchar Publishing House, 1992

Rawat, Ajay S., 'History and Development of the Terai-Bhabar Region', in *Kumaun: Land and People*, ed. K.S. Valdiya, Nainital: Gyanodaya Prakashan, 1988.

Smythies, Olive, *Tiger Lady*, London: William Heinemann, 1953